The Art of Memory in Exile

Hana Píchová

The Art
of Memory in Exile
Vladimir Nabokov
&
Milan Kundera

Southern Illinois University Press
Carbondale & Edwardsville

Library of Congress Cataloging-in-Publication Data
Píchová, Hana, 1961–
The art of memory in exile : Vladimir Nabokov and Milan Kundera / Hana
Píchová.
  p. cm.
Includes bibliographical references and index.
  1. Nabokov, Vladimir Vladimirovich, 1899–1977—Criticism and interpretation.
2. Kundera, Milan—Criticism and interpretation. 3. Exile (Punishment) in
literature. 4. Exiles in literature. 5. Memory in literature. I. Title.

PG3476.N3 Z824 2002
813'.54—dc21

                                                        00-054913
ISBN 0-8093-2396-6 (alk. paper)

The paper used in this publication meets the minimum requirements of
American National Standard for Information Sciences—Permanence of Paper
for Printed Library Materials, ANSI Z39.48-1992. ∞

It is, therefore, a source of great virtue for the practiced mind to learn, bit by bit, first to change about invisible and transitory things, so that afterwards it may be able to leave them behind altogether. The man who finds his homeland sweet is still a tender beginner; he to whom every soil is as his native one is already strong; but he is perfect to whom the entire world is as a foreign land. The tender soul has fixed his love on one spot in the world; the strong man has extended his love to all places; the perfect man has extinguished his.

—Hugo of St. Victor, *Reflections on Exile*

Contents

Acknowledgments

The concept of the other shore is quite familiar to me. By the time this book was completed, half of my life took place on that other shore, a territory once prohibited and only glanced at in cartographic outlines. The leap from the pages of an old tattered atlas to firm ground became a reality on one summer day, a day that displayed all of my parents' free-spiritedness and never-wavering political beliefs. Of course, the leap was a lot more difficult than at first imagined. Too many adventures and memories had already taken place on my native soil. The exilic territory proved to be strangely unfamiliar, as if two-dimensional. Yet the present had to be written; and written it was despite and because of the shadow of the past.

Many people helped me gain understanding of the other shore. With time, my vision became sharper. Dimensions were added, and splendid colors appeared in front of me. I was able to appropriate, even "Pninize" (to use Nabokov's poetic term) my new surroundings. When the time came to write about shores, memory, forgetting, and exile in general, many of the same people were instrumental in that process as well. I would like to thank them for both efforts. Marjorie E. Rhine taught me not only all about the American spirit but also how to formulate my thoughts, which due to personal emotions were occasionally unruly and fragmented. She read the manuscript more than once and offered suggestions that only a truly talented comparativist could. Ronald Harris, Michael Katz, Eric Laursen, Sidney Monas, and Jenifer Presto read parts of the book and offered invaluable advice. Robin Whitaker guided my less than native tongue into a more elegant variety, and the editors of Southern Illinois University Press made the publishing experience a pleasurable one.

I am also grateful for the financial support of the Soros Foundation Research Support Scheme and the Czech Chair Foundation of the University of Texas at Austin. An IREX Short-Term

Travel Grant, offered to me in 1993, when bridging was possible not merely in my imagination, enabled me to retrieve materials and ideas from the past. Perhaps most important, the time required for writing was generously carved out by Michael/Mitch, who for a few years cleared the house of temptingly distracting voices. And when I was lured away, the voices gave me perspective and joy, a gift beyond all. I dedicate this book to those voices of Christopher and Patrick.

I want to thank the *European Studies Journal* for allowing me to include material from a previously published article "The Bowler Hat as a Monument to Time Past in Milan Kundera's *The Unbearable Lightness of Being*," 14, no. 2 (1997): 5–19.

Abbreviations

AE   Robinson, Marc, ed. *Altogether Elsewhere: Writers on Exile.*
New York: Harcourt Brace, 1994.

BLF   Kundera, Milan. *The Book of Laughter and Forgetting.* Trans.
Michael Henry Heim. New York: Harper and Row, 1984.

ENI   Seidel, Michael. *Exile and the Narrative Imagination.* New
Haven: Yale University Press, 1986.

G   Nabokov, Vladimir. *The Gift.* Trans. Michael Scammel
with the collaboration of the author. New York: Vintage
International, 1991.

M   Nabokov, Vladimir. *Mary.* Trans. Michael Glenny with the
collaboration of the author. New York: Vintage International,
1989.

MKF   O'Brien, John. *Milan Kundera and Feminism.* New York: St.
Martin's, 1995.

MW   Said, Edward. "The Mind of Winter: Reflection on Life in
Exile." Harper's, September 1984, 49–55.

N'sEF   Connolly, Julian W. *Nabokov's Early Fiction: Patterns of Self
and Other.* Cambridge: Cambridge University Press, 1992.

N'sO   Alexandrov, Vladimir E. *Nabokov's Otherworld.*
Princeton: Princeton University Press, 1991.

TP   Banerjee, Maria Němcová. *Terminal Paradox: The Novels of
Milan Kundera.* New York: Grove Weidenfield, 1990.

ULB   Kundera, Milan. *The Unbearable Lightness of Being.* Trans. Michael
Henry Heim. New York: Harper and Row, 1984.

UMK   Misurella, Fred. *Understanding Milan Kundera: Public Events, Private
Affairs.* Columbia: University of South Carolina Press, 1993.

VN:RY   Boyd, Brian. *Vladimir Nabokov: The Russian Years.* Princeton:
Princeton University Press, 1990.

Introduction: *Other Shores*

"The Bridge"

I was stiff and cold, I was a bridge, I lay over a ravine. My toes on one side, my fingers clutching the other, I had clamped myself fast into the crumbling clay. The tails of my coat fluttered at my sides. Far below brawled the icy trout stream. No tourist strayed to this impassable height, the bridge was not yet traced on any map. So I lay and waited; I could only wait. Without falling, no bridge, once spanned, can cease to be a bridge.

It was toward evening one day—was it the first, was it the thousandth? I cannot tell—my thoughts were always in confusion and perpetually moving in a circle. It was toward evening in summer, the roar of the stream had grown deeper, when I heard the sound of a human step! To me, to me. Straighten yourself, bridge, make ready, railless beams, to hold up the passenger entrusted to you. If his steps are uncertain, steady them unobtrusively, but if he stumbles show what you are made of and like a mountain god hurl him across to land.

He came, he tapped me with the iron point of his stick, then he lifted my coattails with it and put them in order upon me. He plunged the point of his stick into my bushy hair and let it lie there for a long time, forgetting me no doubt while he wildly gazed around him. But then—I was just following him in thought over mountain and valley— he jumped with both feet on the middle of my body. I shuddered with wild pain, not knowing what was happening. Who was it? A child? A dream? A wayfarer? A suicide? A tempter? A destroyer? And I turned around so as to see him. A bridge to turn around! I had not yet turned quite around when I already began to fall, I fell and in a moment I was torn and transpierced by the sharp rocks which had always gazed up at me so peacefully from the rushing water.[1]

"The Bridge" (1914–17), like most of Franz Kafka's work, raises many puzzling and ultimately indeterminable questions. Is the bridge endowed with animate qualities, human sensations, feelings, and appearance only on some rhetorical or figurative level? Or are we to understand this entity as a literal human being forming his body into a bridge for reasons that are never made clear? A related question might be, Is Gregor Samsa of Kafka's famous story *The Metamorphosis* only metaphorically an insect, or are we to read his transformation as a literal, albeit inexplicable, one? If one thinks of these possibilities—literal, metaphorical—as the two ends of a seesaw, Kafka seems to call on us to maintain a tenuous balance somewhere in the middle, keeping both possibilities open, both poles slightly in motion.[2]

The most well known Czech émigré writer, Milan Kundera, in one of his fictional works, describes exile in terms reminiscent of Kafka's story, explaining that the condition of exile is "a tightrope high above the ground without the net afforded a person by the country where he has his family, colleagues, and friends, and where he can easily say what he has to say in a language he has known from childhood."[3] To live as an émigré is to struggle to maintain a tenuous balance as if at a precarious height; the émigré finds himself or herself on a kind of unstable, rickety bridge between two shores, where the new, unknown territory has to be appropriated and familiarized while the old, known territory becomes the realm of the imaginary.[4] This is a reversal of the émigré's former situation, in which the unknown territory had belonged to the imaginative world. Michael Seidel explains this phenomenon by quoting Søren Kierkegaard's analogy of two neighboring kingdoms, one of which is off limits to the other; the off-limits kingdom is imagined by an inhabitant of the other as being something very different from his own, whether it be terrifying, exotic, or strange (*ENI* 2–3). For an émigré, the "kingdoms" get reversed; the kingdom once so familiar is now relegated to the imaginary, is no longer as familiar. The art of negotiating between these two kingdoms, or—to evoke the bridge more specifically—between the two shores, is a complicated one.[5] This task challenges the powers of the imagination because the émigré must juggle the lure of the potentially suffocating, yet well-known past and the pull of the inevitable forgetting, exacerbated by the pressure to leave behind all that he or she was and to be quickly assimilated into the new present, the new country.[6]

The allure of the past is indeed strong. As Joseph Brodsky points out, an émigré is necessarily a retrospective being, for the native shore is the only known shore, the only territory that is familiar and thus seemingly safe: "Whether pleasant or dismal, the past is always a safe territory, if only because it is already experienced; and the species' capacity to revert, to run backward— especially in its thoughts or dreams, since there we are generally safe as well—is extremely strong in all of us, quite irrespective of the reality we are facing."[7] Yet in this deceptive safety net of the past lies the danger of succumbing solely and obsessively to the task of restoring the past. Again Brodsky's words come to mind: "Retrospection plays an excessive role—compared with other people's lives—in his existence, overshadowing his reality and dimming the future into something thicker than its usual pea soup. Like the false prophets of Dante's *Inferno,* his head is forever turned backward and his tears, or saliva, are running down between his shoulder blades" (*AE* 6). Thus if the émigré retreats utterly into the past, subsiding solely in a realm shaped by memories, then he or she becomes trapped, imprisoned in an illusory world that strips meaning and relevance from the present. Similarly, if the past is idealized or sentimentalized to such an extent that everything the new country has to offer seems inadequate, the émigré is unable to integrate into the new society, is unaccepting of its differences. Edward Said warns against this extreme, for one can make "a fetish of exile, a practice that distances him or her from all connections and commitments."[8]

An understanding or "reading" of the condition of exile reveals as many contradictions, as many twists and turns, as Kafka's strange story and the human bridge itself do. For despite the powerful appeal of turning to the past, which diminishes the possibility of a meaningful existence in the present, it is, ironically, the seemingly opposite phenomenon, the pull of forgetting, that also jeopardizes the art of negotiating the terrain between the two shores, the past and the present. Forgetting enacts a powerful pull on the émigré because, despite the lure of the past, a return trip cannot be literal (on account of political realities) but instead only figurative, only imaginative. Therefore, if imagination is not strong or expansive enough to sustain a creative link with a now necessarily imagined past, an émigré is reduced to clinging desperately to literal memories. Yet specific details about the past begin slowly to slip away, and forgetting becomes an inevitable part of the exilic existence, causing the émigré to lose his or her grip on the old familiar shore.[9]

This forgetfulness can be exacerbated, in certain cases, by what one might call willful forgetting, erasing one's past to fit quickly into the new cultural setting. The problem may arise, according to Said, when there is "pressure on the exile to join— parties, national movements, the state. The exile is offered a new set of affiliations and develops new loyalties. But there is also a loss—of critical perspective, of intellectual reserve, of moral courage" (MW 54). When the native cultural background is abandoned, the émigré is left with none. An émigré, not born and raised in the adoptive culture, will never gain the intense, innate understanding of a native. Thus, in this scenario of willed forgetfulness, the émigré is alienated from both the culture of the homeland and the culture of the adopted country, and the successful balance necessary to maintain one's tenuous position on the rickety bridge of exile is jeopardized.

We can examine the bridge metaphor more directly by returning to Kafka's bizarre short story. Of course, it does not literally describe or portray an émigré, but we should keep in mind that to read Kafka is to keep multiple interpretations at play in a tightrope act that perhaps is always a bit off balance. Certainly on a figurative level, "The Bridge" paints a shocking portrait of the heartrending consequences of a failed attempt to bridge two shores; in fact, upon closer examination, we can see that Kafka's short piece suggests many of the ideas and images central to the experience of exile. But first, a caveat: because the story contains no specific references to the bridge's memory or to its existence before becoming a bridge, the first two problems plaguing émigré experience discussed above, the lure of the past and the tendency to become too obsessed with it, are not of immediate relevance here. However, it is indeed a kind of forgetting that causes the bridge to lose its grip. Also, the bridge relinquishes its own identity by looking backward, and the forced move forward into a new territory, then, becomes something so harsh and seemingly brutal that the bridge is destroyed.

At the beginning of Kafka's short story, the bridge is acutely aware of its remote location, for it occupies a space between two shores of "impassable height." The implication of a difficult access poses a bewildering question: Why was a bridge ever constructed at such a location?[10] The sense of the bridge's geographical dislocation or distance from the known world is intensified by the fact that it is "not yet traced on any map." Because the bridge is not included in, not validated by, a document that would make it known, it exists outside any official affirmation of its identity, as if, like an émigré without a passport or permanent status, its identity is still tenuous, still defined within a liminal space, between two shores. In fact, the bridge clearly recognizes that any identity it does have is integrally connected to or determined by this very liminal status, by its function as a connector between two shores. However, the real test of its "bridgeness," like the measure of success for an émigré, is whether it can successfully serve as a connection between the two shores of crumbling clay: "Without falling, no bridge, once spanned, can cease to be a bridge." This service would begin the bridge's existence, which, thus begun, could then end only by falling.

However, it is not a spontaneous fall that threatens the bridge's existence; it is forgetting that will cause the fall and bring about its demise. For some interminable time, the bridge has been unable to fulfill the very function for which it was designed: "So I lay and waited; I could only wait." But finally someone seeking to cross unexpectedly appears. The passerby arrives on a day that the bridge cannot definitively pin down: "It was toward evening one day—was it the first, was it the thousandth? I cannot tell— my thoughts were always in confusion and perpetually moving in a circle." The bridge's confusion about time points to a lack of memory, revealing a life based on the eternal present moment.

The bridge is not merely plagued by a forgetfulness marked by its inability to record the passage of time; it also performs the quintessential gesture of failed exile, that of physically looking back: "And I turned around. . . . A bridge to turn around! I had not yet turned around when I already began to fall." This tragic turn recalls Brodsky's image, mentioned above, of "the false prophets of Dante's *Inferno*," with heads "forever turned backward." In the case of the bridge, this turn is linked to or caused by forgetting; it forgets that it cannot turn, forgets its function— to span. The bridge, by looking back, loses both itself and presumably all that it tries to carry across with it twisting and falling to its violent death.

The passerby in Kafka's puzzling scenario, on the other hand, might represent what Said warns of, the temptation to move too quickly and wholly into the strangeness of the present, the new country or shore. Despite some initial hesitation—tapping with the iron point of his stick—the passerby does not realize, perhaps, that the bridge is a fragile one, and he jumps too harshly onto its back. His mistake may lie in moving forward too aggressively; he wildly gazes around him, inattentive to the details of the new terrain, forgetting the bridge altogether. He does not gradually merge with the bridge, does not let the bridge help him cross over, as it clearly wishes to do. This mistake costs the traveler his life, as we can presume that he too meets his death on the pointed rocks in the stream below.[11]

Kafka's "Bridge" portrays a tragic, fatal consequence of a failed attempt to cross over treacherous terrain. This eerie outcome opens the text to even more questions and suggests that one answer may lie in the realm of memory. If the bridge had not forgotten its function, it would not have lost its grip. If the passerby had not forgotten the fragility of the bridge at the crucial moment of stepping onto it, he would not have caused the tenuous position of the bridge to fall so horribly askew. To return again to the figurative suggestiveness of the bridge and passerby as they relate to the problems of exile is to see that, to move beyond the risk and dangers of exile in a successful fashion, an émigré must creatively embrace the past while moving forward into a present world full of possibilities.[12]

The creative vision so crucial to a successful negotiation of the chasm that separates the old country from the new is ironically latent within the exilic experience itself, for, as Said points out, the experience of exile can serve as an artistic broadening.

> Most people are principally aware of one culture, one setting, one home; exiles are aware of at least two, and this plurality of vision gives rise to an awareness of simultaneous dimensions, an awareness that—to borrow a phrase from music—is contrapuntal.
>
> For an exile, habits of life, expression, or activity in the new environment inevitably occur against memory of these things in another environment. Thus both the new and the old environment are vivid, actual, occurring together contrapuntally. There is a unique pleasure in this sort of apprehension, especially if the exile is conscious of other contrapuntal juxtapositions that diminish orthodox judgment and elevate appreciative sympathy. There is

also a particular sense of achievement in acting as if one were at home wherever one happens to be. (MW 55)

Such a contrapuntal vision allows both shores to remain in focus at once, a "unique pleasure" that can result in stunning artistry.[13] The present is not disregarded in some obsessive reliance or search for the past but is instead appropriated, made familiar, and appreciated. The past too is not forgotten but instead treasured. This positioning allows the successful émigré, one who maintains a balance on the challenging bridge between past and present, to create a conduit of sorts, one in which the creative spark of the imagination flows freely back and forth between the two shores.[14]

The two authors of exile I deal with in this study, Vladimir Nabokov and Milan Kundera, are extremely successful exemplars of the artistic possibilities inherent in the "plurality of vision" described by Said. These two writers have successfully crossed from one shore to another: the first found an artistic home in Germany, America, and Switzerland after fleeing from postrevolutionary Russia; the other left behind an enforced silence in totalitarian Czechoslovakia to find an increasingly widening audience while writing from his new territory, the shores of France. The remarkable success of these writers of and in exile is even more stunning given that the challenges of exile are especially acute for those who make their living by writing, who must confront, in addition to physical uprootedness, problems of linguistic and cultural differentiation.

Linguistically unhoused, the writer's very being is threatened. How is a writer to proceed in exile: cling to the native language, move into the language of the adopted country, or fall silent? To continue in the mother tongue, in most cases, limits one to a minute audience or to translators' skills, whims, and availability.[15] In addition, torn from its milieu, the language itself undergoes a certain transformation. Vassily Aksyonov sees this variation as a "process of shrinking: from a bubbling ocean, it may turn into a placid pond or, to the contrary, a language which used to be perceived as the fancy amenity of a certain elite may become a gigantic mixture containing all sorts of things."[16]

Yet to abandon the native language—the "protective shell in a forbidding new world" (*AE* xvii)—is to strip oneself of the

uniquely and unequivocally familiar. The writer is essentially bare
when embarking artistically upon another language. The mastery
of new words, phrases, and sentence structures requires dictionaries and editors and still can result in unpredictable outcomes.
Language, the very means of creation, can become a secondary,
blunt tool. Coming to this realization alone is daunting, humili-
ating, even marginalizing. Breyten Breytenbach puts it succinctly:
"You live in an acquired linguistic zone like going dressed in the
clothes of the husband of your mistress."[17] Of course, this frustration is not shared by all writers. Eva Hoffman has a positive
outlook on the acquisition of a new language, for despite its difficulties and mysteries it offers "borderless possibilities."[18] And
indeed, without either the native or the newly acquired words,
no possibilities come into view.

The option not to write results in silence, solitude, and ironically an acceptance of one's own banishment. After all, exile is
implemented as a form of the most severe censure, a swift sword
meant to obliterate verbal power. For a once-active writer, to
respond with a blank page is to confirm and participate in personal and public forgetting. Silence erases the person from the
collective memory of those left behind on the native shore and
prevents him or her from ever being recognized by the inhabitants of the new shore. Silence, moreover, diminishes personal
memory, inasmuch as writing provides for a recovery of past
mementos via an imaginary journey back home, when physically
such a return is impossible. According to Robinson: "Exiles can
travel back and forth between two languages, or two versions of
the same language, retrieving ideas left behind (those that can
only be expressed in native speech) and venturing deeper into a
new land than they could on foot" (*AE* xvii).[19]

Still, if the exiled writer chooses words, native or adopted,
there lurks another adversity, one that is culturally grounded.
Stanisław Barańczak forewarns of the cultural differences: "The
audience in the exiled writer's adopted country, even if not entirely indifferent, is often unable to understand not merely his
interpretations of reality but simply what he is speaking about.
And quite naturally so, since neither the material of the reader's
own experiences nor their inherited way of viewing reality has
prepared them to accept this sort of a literary world" (*AE* 248).
Misreadings of humor, phrases, commands, and sexual and political implications are inevitable. Should the writer mechanisti-

cally explain that which is painfully obvious to the fellow émigré audience, so that the foreign reader can feel part of the text? Or should misunderstanding and perplexity be expected and accepted as one of the many realities of exile? And even if a delicate balance is achieved—just enough of the original flavor is cut out to be better understood—is not the writer forlornly removed from the newly adopted culture? As Barańczak points out, "Being, after all, an outsider in the culture he is trying to conquer, the writer sooner or later realizes that some of this culture's qualities are lost on him as well" (244). The cultural displacement, in fact, can be a double one.

Despite these challenges, Kundera and Nabokov have been more than merely successful in dealing with the disadvantages of exile; they have showcased this apprehension in brilliant fashion, to great acclaim. Their works are part of the Western canon (regularly included in the syllabi of many university courses); they have obtained massive readership; and their works have been translated into numerous languages, as well as adapted to film.[20] The reason for this phenomenal success may be tied to both Nabokov's and Kundera's advantage in knowing the language of the other shore before they were faced with the challenges of the unfamiliar territories in which they found themselves after exile. In addition, each had a good cultural knowledge of the country that was to be his new home. Nabokov's family traveled extensively, and English nannies and German tutors were an integral part of his upbringing. Kundera also carried this advantage with him into exile, for French culture and literature were his interest and love long before he found his way to France. Thus, for both Nabokov and Kundera, the other shore was perhaps not as terrifying, for the imagined "kingdom," to recall Kierkegaard, was already at least partly a familiar land.

Because of this background, Nabokov and Kundera were more easily able to develop the contrapuntal vision in which countries, shores, and languages are held in a dual focus; moreover, they were able to explore and extend this vision even further by laying bare, in their fiction, the very devices by which they achieved this vision. In the novels I discuss in this study, the first novel written by each man in exile *(Mary* and *The Book of Laughter and Forgetting)* and the novel that might be considered each man's magnum opus *(The Gift* and *The Unbearable Lightness of Being),* these authors create what we might think of as novelistic kaleidoscopes. *Kaleidoscope* is indeed an apt image to use here because the Greek roots of this word, *kalos* (beautiful), *eidos* (form), and *skopein* (view), suggest that it is through an artful view or perspective of fragments that a beautiful form emerges.[21] We might imagine the mirrors that form the reflecting surfaces of the kaleidoscope to be the shimmering surfaces of the present (the new shore at which the émigré writer has arrived), while the fragments of colored glass are the pieces of the past—not only pieces of a personal nature but also, especially for a writer, the pieces of a cultural mosaic that he or she carries into exile. A careful turn of the kaleidoscope sends the glass fragments, the pieces of the cultural and personal past, tumbling into a constellation of surprising beauty, but a turn that is too sudden or too fast (like the one taken by Kafka's bridge) leaves the pieces fallen into a shapeless heap, dull because they lose their form and are no longer illuminated by the light playing off the mirrors. For Nabokov and Kundera, then, a crucial key to both their artistry and their success is memory.[22]

Consequently, the plots and narrative structures of the works I discuss in this book are determined by the ever-present personal and cultural recollections of key fictional characters. Fragments of old letters, tattered photographs, sentimental possessions, occasional smells, and visual remembrances of native countryside are scattered throughout the texts as props for the heroes' personal recalls. These flashes from the past afflict individual characters, more or less, unexpectedly, poignantly, having the capacity either to disturb or to enrich the present. On the other hand, cultural memory, primarily composed of historical, political, and literary detours, is intentionally evoked by fictional writers and intellectuals, to re-evaluate, appreciate, even better understand one's heritage from the newly gained across-the-border perspective.[23] In short, personal and cultural recollections, whether fictional or real, serve not only as a sword against forgetting but allow for uniquely individual plots and forms to take shape.

The structure of the four chapters presented here is as follows: the first two chapters explore the presentation of the challenges of piecing together fragments of personal memory; the last two deal with cultural memory. Two chapters, one on personal and one on cultural memory, are devoted to each author. Each chapter is split into three sections: section one deals with the first novels written in exile (*Mary* in Nabokov's chapter and *The Book of Laughter and Forgetting* in Kundera's), the ones that afford the first view into the kaleidoscope of exile. Section two offers a reading of how issues raised in the first novels receive much more elaborate patterning in the later pivotal novels of exile (*The Gift* by Nabokov and *The Unbearable Lightness of Being* by Kundera), which display a masterful turn of the kaleidoscopic art. This sophisticated patterning is closely explored in the third section of each chapter by an examination of the narrative structures employed by Nabokov and Kundera in these pivotal novels. Through complicated twists and turns of structures, images, and themes, these writers create a masterful blend of personal and cultural memory, bringing together the pieces of their pasts in unique fashion.

In their virtuoso displays of literary talent, Nabokov and Kundera lay bare the very device by which they have succeeded as émigrés: a creative constellation of past and present, fused through the powers of the imagination that bring personal memory and cultural memory into stunning juxtaposition. In the novels considered here, the importance of this strategy for success is foregrounded through portrayals of fictional émigrés who fail creatively to bridge the present and past and the consequences of their failure and through descriptions of those who imaginatively utilize the resources and riches of the past to move forward into the future or to acquire an artistic vision that allows them to transcend the challenges and difficulties of exile. Kundera provides the best examples of fictional émigrés who fail to sustain a rich personal memory that would allow for the possibility of a contrapuntal vision that creatively recuperates the past and who consequently come to lead reductive, devalued lives. Although Nabokov possesses such characters as well, his most memorable ones are those émigrés who rely on their personal histories to restore physical strength and stability or to enrich a present that at times seems mundane, devoid of creative outlets.

Both writers emphasize the importance of cultural memory as well, although they do so in different ways. The protagonist of Nabokov's *Gift*, a young writer, returns to his cultural past in his rereadings and appropriations of the most influential nineteenth-century Russian writers. Yet he not only positions his voice within this rich tradition of the past but also carries its resonances, its tones, into the unfamiliar present. This act enables

him to gain a new, even appreciative outlook on his present condition. Exile thus emerges as a meeting place where different
cultures converge, allowing for a broader, more expansive aesthetic to develop as a fertile ground where creative imagination
is able to transcend all physical and political boundaries. In
Kundera's *Unbearable Lightness of Being,* photography becomes a
means of exploring cultural memory. The photograph is presented as a powerful record that documents and preserves, yet
one that, when manipulated or doctored, rewrites—even obliterates—reality. Thus, cultural memory can be formed and manipulated simply by a two-dimensional image, an image that turns
out to be dangerously ambiguous. Through photography,
Kundera promotes and celebrates an essential questioning that
refuses to accept any given truth as the only truth, a questioning fostered by an artistic vision that rips through the boundaries
of the mimetic.

The profound significance of personal and cultural memory
is investigated on the philosophical and thematic levels of the
novels studied here, and later it is mirrored in the intricate structural patterns of the subsequent novels, *The Gift* and *The Unbearable Lightness of Being.* In the case of *The Gift,* the complex process of the young protagonist's artistic development is reflected
in the ornate literary structure of the novel: the seemingly fragmented sections, when recognized in the enforceable pattern of
a spiral in a circle, enrich the reader's own perspicacity. In the case
of the narrative structure of *The Unbearable Lightness of Being,* the
play of repetition results in a fragmented, achronological text that
cannot be easily apprehended unless the reader enacts a kind of
personal memory of his or her own reading experience and is
always alert to repeated terms, images, and ideas vis-à-vis their
earlier appearances. This reading strategy affords the reader a
better glimpse into the kaleidoscopic vision of the novel, a
chance to see the seeming fragments fall into a stunning pattern.
The structure of both novels not only evokes a reading experience that ideally mirrors the creative strategies necessary for
success in exile but also says much about the power of fiction.
In *The Gift,* the protagonist's critical framing (within the stanzas
of an inverted circular sonnet) of his biography of the radical
critic Nikolay Gavrilovich Chernyshevsky (whose political radi-
calism and conservative aesthetics are direct antecedents of
Vladimir Ilich Lenin's political tyranny and the aesthetic doctrine

of socialist realism) suggests the limitations, even dangers, of utilitarian, merely mimetic apprehension and representation. Kundera calls upon a broader history of the novel, defining it as a genre of questioning, placing his own work into a broad sweep of the history of the novel as a kind of bridge, as a way of preserving a spirit of questioning that resists accepting any one truth as the only truth. Ultimately, both Nabokov and Kundera warn against seeing the world from only one perspective. Their vision is a kaleidoscopic one, one that is enriched by the other shores and the ever-shifting fragments of personal and cultural memory, creating unexpected patterns that in turn allow for a new view, a new reading, a new interpretation.

Part One: *Personal Memory*

We children had gone down to the village, and it is when I recall that particular day that I see with the utmost clarity the sun spangled river; the bridge,
the dazzling tin of a can left by a fisherman on its wooden railing; the lin-
den-treed hill with its rosy-red church and marble mausoleum where my
mother's dead reposed; the dusty road to the village; the strip of short,
pastel-green grass, with bald patches of sandy soil, between the road and
the lilac bushes behind which walleyed, mossy log cabins stood in a rickety
row; the stone building of the new schoolhouse near the wooden old one;
and, as we swiftly drove by, the little black dog with very white teeth that
dashed out from among the cottages at a terrific pace but in absolute
silence, saving his voice for the brief outburst he would enjoy when his
muted spurt would at last bring him close to the speeding carriage.

—Vladimir Nabokov, *Speak, Memory*

1. Vladimir Nabokov: *Variations on a Butterfly*

Nabokov's first novel, *Mary* (1926), written only a few years after the writer's own exile, opens predictably with an émigré setting of a pension "both Russian and nasty"[1] in the midst of Berlin: Russian, because it is inhabited by people derailed from their homeland owing to the tragic force of the Bolshevik revolution; nasty, because the pension is so close to the railroad that its walls shake and rattle as if a train were going through it. The marginality of this place, associated both figuratively and literally with a state of transit, mirrors the physical and existential instability of the émigrés who live within its walls. For these Russian "wanderers"—the word *exile* derives from the etymologically related Greek word *alasthai*, which means "to wander"— exile provides no peace; exile is like a railroad, "a mere locus of movement, or at best a station where people only kill time between a place they remember coming from and a destination they do not know."[2] And while the émigrés cling forlornly to the hope of returning to Russia, their wandering is not the far-too-long journey of Odysseus back to his homeland on the shores of Ithaca. Rather, it is a search for stability on foreign soil.

As if to fulfill the hope of his displaced fellow countrymen, one of the lodgers of the pension, Ganin, sets upon a journey directed backward to his place of remembrance, to Russia. For a Russian émigré, such an expedition would be virtually impossible without dire consequences at the time of the novel's setting, 1924, so he resorts to personal memory, to a mental revisitation of a precious time and place of his past. This way, Ganin is able to soar over political and geographical boundaries and safely return to his lost homeland. However, Ganin's imaginative journey proves not to be a smooth ride into the past but a chaotic return, experienced by him and represented for the reader in bits and pieces, seemingly scattered flashes from his past. At first, it seems to provide little escape or solace from his present unstable and fragmented environment. But by the end of the novel, this journey, created out of personal memories, does lead to a new direction for Ganin, to a "secret turning point for him, an awakening" (*M* 113), an awakening that unexpectedly results in finding more permanence in exile.

The unstable and rootless present condition of Berlin in which Ganin finds himself is evident both in the constant shaking to which the pension is subject because of passing trains and in the dispersed arrangement of the pension's interior, where most of the action takes place. Deliberately and precisely laid out for the reader is a long hallway, which contains six bedrooms, each labeled in sequence with year-old calendar pages dating from 1 April to 6 April 1923. The German landlady's method of distinguishing individual doors by outdated, torn-off pages reflects the émigrés' own existential situation. Forcefully torn out of their once-whole country, these lodgers now have become displaced fragments. And when the befittingly labeled doors are opened, the émigrés' uprootedness is revealed even further. Each of the rooms is equipped with furniture that at one time formed a unified household but now has become separated, haphazardly placed here and there like a "dismembered skeleton's bones" (6), to furnish a residence for the equally displaced lodgers. Ironically, it is in this least stable and least inspiring of environments, within the confines of the pension, where an unexpected discovery is made, one that causes "the entire kaleidoscope of [Ganin's] life to shift" and to bring back "the past to overwhelm him" (30).

The first door in the narrow hallway of the pension, labeled 1 April, forebodes something of the unexpected, if not an April Fools' joke. And indeed it is in this room, within a large desk of a truly unusual appearance, "an oaken monster with a cast-iron inkwell in the form of a toad and with a middle drawer as deep as a ship's hold" (6), where Ganin's past world, represented by a photograph of his first love, a young woman named Mary, lies hidden.[3] Following the discovery of this photograph, Ganin's recollections and memories come flowing "after many years of humdrum oblivion" (*M* 27) and trigger a journey into "a world that had perished" (33), where a love affair once took place. It is not only the contents of the desk that warrant our attention but also the "oaken monster" itself. After all, no other piece of furniture in the pension is described in such a curious and precise manner. The desk may be taken for a symbol of what is to come, of the journey itself, for its overly poetic depiction hints at the poetic nature of Ganin's return to the past. The incongruous images (monster, toad, ship's hold) foreshadow the images that surface from the past, the scattered or fragmented images that do not seem to fit together. Finally, the desk foretells that something unexpected, the monstrous exterior, will yield something precious, just as Ganin's imaginative return to the past will suddenly propel him out of the stagnant pension.

After the detailed description of the desk's appearance, it is surprising that the photograph of Mary, the catalyst of Ganin's journey, becomes available to Ganin and the reader's gaze only after a delay, and even then her portrait is never drawn in full. Ganin comes upon the photograph only after the current owner of the desk, Alfyorov, who happens to be Mary's husband, retrieves some old photos from the drawer while talking excitedly about Mary's anticipated arrival in Berlin, which is to take place in four days. We are told that at first Ganin looks without much interest at the photographs handed to him by Alfyorov. His gaze stops on the image of a woman "with a merry, very toothy mouth" (25), a woman who turns out to be not Alfyorov's wife but his sister. The momentary deception is quickly corrected and another photo is produced, "a poor snapshot, but quite a good likeness all the same. And here's another, taken in our garden. Mary's the one sitting, in the white dress" (25). Only then does Ganin react, by abruptly leaving the room. Ganin's sudden departure puzzles both Alfyorov and the reader, for at this point in the text the reader does not know that Ganin had a relationship with Mary nine years earlier. Moreover, the missing portrayal of Mary—compounded by our view of Alfyorov's sister, who, although superfluous in the novel, is presented here in greater detail—opens up another lacuna in the text, creating more suspense as the reader wonders not only about Ganin's abrupt response but also about who Mary is and what she looks like.[4]

The deferred revelation and description of Mary's persona mirror Ganin's deliberate delay in re-creating the details of his love affair with her. In other words, Ganin's personal journey into the past is not presented as a linear return. Instead, it occurs in a piecemeal, fragmented fashion, as though the fragmentation of the present, his life in exile, permeates the world of his past. The images come back to Ganin and are recounted for the reader only in small flashes—a hair bow like a butterfly, a sweet kiss on a young woman's throat—as if they were the result of an old, patched-together reel of film fed fitfully through a projector. The possible reasons for the fragmentary way in which these memories surface are many. Human memory functions according to sometimes seemingly random connections, jumps, and flashes. Furthermore, Ganin desires to approach Mary as he did nine years before, again just as a first-time lover would, privileging and lingering pleasurably over certain details or fragments that are important to him alone. In addition, Ganin's present environment, the unstable, noisy pension, and his lifestyle, that of an émigré living out of suitcases, surely provides him with no solid ground from which to reconstruct his past in a leisurely and linear fashion.

However, before Ganin can approach the world of his past, he must clear away obstacles from the present that block and occupy his mental space and physically deprive him of strength by tying him to his humdrum world. According to Henri Bergson, "To call up the past in the form of an image, we must be able to withdraw ourselves from the action of the moment, we must have the power to value the useless, we must have the will to dream."[5] The world of the past starts to emerge only after Ganin tells his current girlfriend, from whom he has long wanted to break, that things are over between them. Soon after this breakup, he stretches out on a park bench and, feeling expansive and free, begins to dream, to "listen" to his "gentle companion," his "gray shadow." This shadowy doppelgänger plays a number of functions within the novel: it is tied to Ganin's role as an extra in a film, and it can be seen as an example of what Julian Connolly calls "an embryonic model of the author-character bifurcation," fully developed only in Nabokov's later novels.[6] It may also reflect the Bergsonian process of recalling memories: "Whenever we are trying to recover a recollection, to call up some period of our history, we become conscious of an act *sui generis* by which we detach ourselves from the present in order to replace ourselves, first, in the past in general, then, in a certain region of the past— a work of adjustment, something like the focusing of a camera."[7] Most important for my discussion, however, is the doppelgänger's connection to the representation of Ganin's physical self, which mirrors the émigré's split, a split between the lost homeland and the country of exile.

As the novel begins, this physical self has clearly deteriorated—Ganin is no longer himself, not the man he used to be. Before, in Russia, he was able to "walk on his hands, quite as well as a Japanese acrobat . . . pick up a chair with his teeth . . . break a string by flexing his biceps" (*M* 8). However, now in exile, he feels as if "some bolt had worked loose inside him, he had acquired a stoop and he admitted to Podtyagin [a fellow boarder] that he was suffering from insomnia 'like a nervous female'" (8). Also he sits huddled and naked, thinking that putting on clothes is akin to dressing up like a ridiculous circus poodle. It is as if he left his physical strength and spirit in Russia, while into exile he brought only an empty body shell, which now aimlessly occupies space.[8] Physically divided between the two countries, he is neither here nor there. But immediately following the discovery of Mary's photograph, as he prepares to revisit his homeland, the active physical self suddenly reemerges: he "jumps" out of bed the next morning "with a determined sweep," feels that "he had become exactly nine years younger," smiles "with joy" as he douses his body with cold water and dresses quickly (*M* 28). This transformation signals that through memory Ganin's strength can be retrieved, can be transported into the new territory of exile. Ganin thus can unite his body shell and his strength and become whole again.

Ganin's renewed physical strength and energy go hand in hand with a sense of control over his mental capacities. No longer spiritless, bored, and depressed, he is able to take charge of the unfolding recollections. In fact, the seemingly fragmentary presentation derives from the working of memory, his present situation, and his desire to approach Mary slowly as if to honor her, but paradoxically it also demonstrates a thought-out creative process, a highly artful and determined control over the imaginary world he evokes. As Connolly points out, although "the scenes Ganin re-creates are meant to represent actual experience, the manner in which they are stitched together seems suspiciously polished and refined, more like a calculated work of art than the real flow of personal memory" (*N'sEF* 39–40).[9] Ganin's own words confirm this view. He states that the best memories depend on a deliberate mental technique and not on chance inspiration. The mental technique is linked to artistry, as is evident from Ganin's following description of his reverie to a fellow lodger, the aged poet Podtyagin: "I started a wonderful affair" (*M* 43), for the Russian word *roman* means both "affair" and "novel."[10] And indeed he has started both. When Ganin begins to recall the past, he wanders through Berlin completely self-

absorbed, oblivious to his surroundings: "On the street he care-
lessly bumped into people and once a fast car braked hard and
swore, having nearly hit him" (*M* 33). It is as if he is experiencing falling in love for the first time all over again. At the same
time, he is involved in a complicated, conscious process of se-
lecting and repositioning images and fragments of memories, a
process that reveals both mental sharpness and the creative tem-
perament necessary in any literary endeavor:

> He was a god, re-creating a world that perished. Gradually
> he resurrected that world, to please the girl whom he did
> not dare to place in it until it was absolutely complete. But
> her image, her presence, the shadow of her memory de-
> manded that in the end he must resurrect her too—and
> he intentionally thrust away her image, as he wanted to
> approach it gradually, step by step, just as he had done
> nine years before. Afraid of making a mistake, of losing
> his way in the bright labyrinth of memory, he re-created
> his past life watchfully, fondly, occasionally turning back
> for some forgotten piece of trivia, but never running
> ahead too fast. (33)[11]

But why does Ganin need to approach his personal past with
such creativity? After all, he is not motivated by literary ambitions, nor does he seek an audience to show off his artistry. Perhaps Ganin intuits that his aesthetic sense is his preservation, for
it prevents him from falling into a potentially entrapping past.
A dialogue between Podtyagin and Klara reveals that indeed the
past can be a "dangerous" territory:

> "If we were in Russia, Klarochka, some country doctor or
> a well-to-do architect would be courting you. Tell me—do
> you love Russia?"
> "Very much."
> "Quite so. We should love Russia. Without the love of
> us émigrés, Russia is finished. None of the people there
> love her."
> "I'm already twenty-six," said Klara, "I type all morn-
> ing, and five times a week I work until six. I get very tired.
> I'm quite alone in Berlin. What do you think, Anton
> Sergeyevich—will it go on like this for long?" (*M* 53–54)

Their exchange discloses an idealization of Russia, or what Said terms "a fetish of exile" (MW 54). Podtyagin assumes that Klara would be much better off in Russia, where surely a successful marriage would come about to bring both financial security and good social standing. Although such an outlook was quite realistic in the nineteenth century, now in the early 1920s, given the changes the country has been through, the Bolshevik revolution and the Civil War, Klara's prospects would be rather dim. Podtyagin's loss of perspective, however, is not the only thing responsible for his nostalgia. Memories of Russia keep unexpectedly, frequently, and without warning invading his present Berlin life: "'Life's freer—and cheaper, apparently,' said Podtyagin [referring to France], spooning up an unmelted scrap of sugar and thinking that there was something Russian about that little porous lump, something rather like the melting snow in springtime" (*M* 54). These interjections seem at first harmless, perhaps only sentimental fragments, plaguing the character in his present existence. However, his lack of control over these thoughts eventually results in Podtyagin's losing his passport, acquired with great difficulty, just when he is describing a dream about Russia to Ganin. This in turn results in the loss of an escape route from Germany to the freer and cheaper France, where his niece (the only relative he has in exile) is waiting for him. In other words, Podtyagin is unable to reach his final destination (Germany to him represents only a transit station), is unable to settle down in exile, because of a very distant, very nebulous past. He becomes literally trapped in the pension.[12]

Klara, after listening to Podtyagin's views on what could have been, presents her current situation in sharp contrast: her endlessly repetitive existence, typing day in and day out, leaves her with nothing but alienation and monotony and slim prospects of a good marriage.[13] Because she takes no action to change this meaningless present, she is doomed to remain eternally in what Ganin terms the "house of ghosts" (*M* 114). Both Podtyagin and Klara indulge in the idealization of the past, one of them overrun by memories; the other, by passivity. Unable to understand or adapt to the present situation, they are reduced to living like ghosts. In Podtyagin's case, this metaphor becomes literal, for as the novel ends he is seen suffering from yet another heart attack, this time a fatal one.

As already stated, Ganin's reverie differs in both manner and result. He is not merely a passenger on his journey, not just a passive recipient of memories; he is a navigator who actively manipulates them. His control over the potentially dangerous stream of memories, over the entrapping past, can be detected from the outset of his journey, for he decides on a precise structure for his reverie, almost as if he were creating a literary piece. His organization is based on first resurrecting that perished world, and not "until it was absolutely complete" would he bring Mary to life. This structure is not only adhered to but also finalized with a specific goal in mind. Once Mary becomes mentally re-created, Ganin plans to step out of his reverie, his past, and walk to the train station where she is due to arrive: "He would take her far away, he would work tirelessly for her." In other words, Ganin is planning to steal Mary away from Alfyorov. This desire to abandon memories for reality, an imaginary love affair for a real one, shows Ganin's unwillingness to sentimentally indulge in his memories forever.[14] He is not asking what could have been but what will be. Thus Ganin's journey is a recuperative one. As already stated, his initial preparations, his consultation with his doppelgänger, restore his physical strength. And the deliberately creative and structured manner in which he plunges into the past provides him with mental clarity, which in turn ensures him a route back out of the past and ultimately out of the stagnant pension. Ganin's journey into the past is therefore one that restores his physical strength and his flagging spirits.

Appropriately, the images that surface first during Ganin's imaginative journey are those that foreshadow his recuperation, for they are linked to his recovery from a teenage bout of typhus. Leona Toker makes an interesting observation about typhus in this novel. Typhus may be "the Pandora's box of memories," for when Alfyorov produces a photograph of his sister who had died of typhus along with Mary's photo, Ganin's memories are set into motion.[15] In the following scene, again it is typhus that brings back detailed memories; this time, Ganin's bed and wallpaper design emerge in precise contours: "One would fashion people's profiles out of these roses or wander up and down with one's eyes, trying not to touch a single flower or a single leaf on the way, finding gaps in the pattern, wriggling through, doubling back, landing in a blind alley and starting one's journey through the luminous maze all over again" (*M* 32). Ganin's precise recall of his preoccupation with creating profiles and finding his way through the flowery maze on the wallpaper, in essence, is a symbolic representation of his current journey, which is based on re-creating a loved one and finding a way out of the entrapping pattern of exile. In addition, the reason his previous experience with illness serves as the starting place for the journey back to Mary is that "in this room, where Ganin had recuperated at six-teen, was conceived that happiness, the image of that girl he was to meet in real life a month later" (32). Even though Ganin him-self realizes that, of course, this was only a "boyish premoni-tion," he feels on this morning after seeing the photograph that "never had such a premonition been so completely fulfilled" (33). The pattern of first indulging in the pleasure of conceiving an image, fostered in the original scenario when Ganin the teenager hears of Mary's sweetness from a young medical student before he himself has even seen her, is echoed the second time around in that he savors the task of visualizing memories of Mary in a slow, pleasurable way as he waits the four days until her planned arrival in Berlin. Even the weakness he felt after the bout of ty-phus is reexperienced—and doubly so, for Ganin's pleasantly aching legs from his long walk around Berlin, a walk inspired by his reverie after seeing the photograph of Mary, remind him of his boyhood sickness: "Wandering around Berlin on that Tues-day in Spring, he recuperated all over again, felt what it was like to get out of bed for the first time, felt the weakness in his legs" (33). In other words, his shade of the present is slowly becom-ing connected with the spirit of the past.

These first images foreshadow not only the recuperative na-ture of the journey but also its fragmentary presentation. In the beginning, we get flashes of Ganin's environment—the coun-try house, the wallpaper design—as well as his mental state. The fragmentary nature of these memories is highlighted stylistically in the sentences used, which are incomplete, fragments them-selves: "Nine years ago. Summer of 1915, a country house, ty-phus" (31). And when Mary starts emerging, like a butterfly from a chrysalis, it is in the same synecdochic manner as the overall re-creation. The first time Ganin sees her in his youth is from behind; while sitting in a barn converted into a site for festive musical performance, he notices the black bow that decorates her hair, fluttering like a butterfly in front of his eyes. The second time—"he could not remember when it was that he saw her next, whether it was the following day or a week later" (47)—the reader is allowed access to a slightly more detailed description of Mary.

Approaching with Ganin on his bicycle through the idyllic countryside, we get a glimpse of her blue skirt, jacket, and white blouse, but the only thing we and Ganin see fully as he quickly rides by is again the black bow: "As Ganin caught up with her, like a soft breeze, he saw only the folds of blue stuff stretching and rippling across her back, and the black silk bow like two outstretched wings" (48). He compares this bow to a Camberwell Beauty.[16] The lepidopteral allusion fittingly describes how Mary appears to him at the beginning of their relationship.[17] The Camberwell Beauty, *Nymphalis antiopa* (Nymphalidae), is a visually spectacular butterfly—velvety in texture, wings of dark brown with creamy borders—but difficult to catch, for few can be found. In fact, it is because Mary seems to be in constant motion that Ganin is unable to catch up with her, rendering our initial view of her incomplete. Although Ganin eventually does observe her Tatar eyes and "adorable mobile eyebrows, a dark complexion with a covering of very fine, lustrous down which gave a specially warm tinge to her cheeks," this close proximity within their relationship does not last long. Ganin is forced to leave from the countryside, and an agonizingly frustrating "snowbound era of their love" begins, frustrating because the lovers cannot see each other often enough or find privacy when they do meet. Ganin is like a butterfly hunter both then and now. In the past, he captured only occasional sights of Mary and even more rarely found opportunities to meet with her. Now, in exile, he is recapturing the selected pieces of his past with the net of his memory.

In his present, in the dreary Berlin pension, however, a few tangible fragments of Mary already exist, shedding further light on Ganin's past. Ganin's suitcase contains several letters that he and Mary exchanged following their love affair. Because Ganin was obviously limited in what he could take into exile, his decision to select an object of no practical value reveals not only the importance of the love affair to him but also his need to carry at least a part of his past with him at all times.[18] The letters, like everything else connected with Ganin's present and past, are displayed in fragmented form. These fragments are samples of the wartime correspondence that passed between Ganin and Mary like "Cabbage butterfl[ies] flying over the trenches." Here the lepidopteral reference seems quite ambiguous. On the one hand, it is a hauntingly beautiful image of a white and fluttering thing, like a sign of surrender and peace, over the trenches of death and war. Perhaps, then, this image suggests that their fragile letters, missives flying across the gulf or trench that separates the lovers, will be ultimately as insignificant as butterflies amidst warfare. Or, as Joann Karges points out, the image contains "a shade of symbolism of the transcendent spirit in a white butterfly"; in other words, the butterflies represent the souls of displaced persons in a foreign land.[19] On the other hand, the Cabbage butterfly, unlike the Camberwell Beauty, appears frequently and possesses none of the spectacular markings of the Camberwell. And indeed the few lines available to us from Mary's letters prove not so "rare" or "spectacular"; instead, they reveal a lack of intellect, emotional depth, and even close affinity to Alfyorov through the misuse of the same word: "Today it's so boring, boring. It's such a pity that the days go by so pointlessly and stupidly—and these are supposed to be the best, the happiest years of our life. It looks as if I shall soon turn into a hypocrite—I mean, hypochondriac" (*M* 92). The lines indicate why the relationship had not continued. In the present setting, these epistolary fragments may also serve to forewarn Ganin of oversentimentalization and overidealization not only of the entire affair but of the past in general. Podtyagin's tragic fate, as already discussed, exemplifies the danger of losing a realistic perspective of the past.

As Ganin recalls, his first prolonged encounter with Mary, the first time he talked to her, occurred in a pavilion with multicolored windows (56), a kaleidoscope of sorts, offering a fragmented vision. Ganin has chosen to look through the window into the past for a four-day tumble through this kaleidoscope of nostalgia, believing that the past can return and that he will be able to regain Mary. As it turns out, the outcome is quite different from what he expects: he captures not Mary but his own self. Physically, he becomes a whole being, no longer followed by his shadowy doppelgänger, no longer split. When his strength returns, he feels "light and free as though he were about to fly away" (114), which he does by leaving the pension, heading off to the train station. Mentally, at the end of the novel, he has awakened, gained a new outlook: "And just as the sun rose higher and the shadows dispersed to their usual places, so in that sober light the world of memories in which Ganin had dwelt became what it was in reality: the distant past" (113). As he notices a new house being built, which as yet has no windows, affording him a clear, untainted gaze into the morning light, he realizes "with merciless clarity that his affair with Mary was ended forever" (114). Mary belongs to his past, which now includes the Russian pension. Thus, just as the unexpected discovery of a photograph in an "oaken monster" revived personal memories and thus propelled Ganin on an imaginative journey into his past, so now the new physical and mental self he gains from this revisitation allows him to set out on a real journey. This journey, away from the fragmented, shaky world of Berlin, to France—where in Podtyagin's words everything is cheaper and freer—promises more stability, perhaps even a homeland. Enriched with the Camberwell Beauty of the past, his butterfly net is now ready for captures of the future.

In *The Gift* (1937–38), exile is no longer depicted as a railroad station "where people only kill time between a place they remember coming from and a destination they do not know" (*VN:RY* 246). The destination has now been reached. The protagonist, Fyodor Godunov-Cherdyntsev, is not trying to escape Berlin, as Ganin once did. He is at home here, moving skillfully through Berlin's complex system of streets, whether only browsing or on his way to give language lessons. In Brian Boyd's words, "never again would [Nabokov] re-create in such exhaustive detail a city's parks and squares, its offices and shops, its buses and streetcars, its modes and mores" (*VN:RY* 464). The emphasis on the protagonist's external realm and the entire city, rather than on the internal world of the pension and only fragments of Berlin as depicted in *Mary,* signals that the protagonist now belongs to this environment, an environment that is presented in its entirety. It signals that he has achieved physical stability in his new surroundings. Although there are still frequent physical relocations in *The Gift,* from one pension to another, they are caused by Fyodor's writing habits, which do not make him an ideal or desirable lodger, rather than by his unstable émigré existence. Despite this relative stability in *The Gift,* Fyodor is presented as a wanderer. However, his wandering is characterized by a journey for a voice, a voice that can sustain artistic talent in exile, outside the cultural and linguistic boundaries of Russia. Fyodor is a writer whose journey into the past is initiated not by a chance discovery from within a desk drawer but by a deliberate act of penmanship.

In *The Gift*, the focus on artistic issues, rather than on the mere concerns of settling down in exile so poignantly described in *Mary*, is understandable, given that more than ten years have passed between the writing of the two novels. The author, like Fyodor, is physically well-grounded in exile.[20] The trains that once shook "the nasty Russian pension" and carried Mary to Berlin, the trains that symbolized the hope that perhaps one distant day a return to the homeland would be possible, do not appear in *The Gift*. The accomplished physical stability now also needs to be united with artistic stability. The primary concern has switched to that of becoming a great writer, one Russia has never seen, one who succeeds in exile. And although Nabokov had achieved prominence among the small yet sagacious Russian émigré audience, in the 1930s his work remained virtually unknown in the West. Nabokov's resolution that *The Gift* would be his last novel written in Russian shows that he wanted to expand his reading public and therefore make exile not only his physical home but also his artistic home. Thus, on the one hand, *The Gift* is the author's farewell to his native linguistic artistry; on the other, it is an act of preparation for broadening his audience beyond the restrictively small group of émigré readers, an act of expansion for a voice to be fully heard in exile. This expansion is governed by the upcoming switch to the English language, as well as by an exploration of the artistic theme itself. This exploration is described as the protagonist's journey into both personal and cultural memories of his past, a past that gives this voice its undeniable uniqueness beyond the borders of his homeland.

The importance of journey as a theme is evident from the start. Moving scenes open and close this novel, much as the way in which the imaginative journey that occurs in *Mary* is framed by Ganin's intention to leave the shaking pension and Berlin (which opens the novel and instigates an anticipated journey) and his departure for France at the end. One important difference, however, is that in *The Gift* the moving scenes are accompanied by Fyodor's thoughts about his future poetic creations, thoughts that reveal an artist at work. The novel opens with a detailed description of a moving van being met by a Russian émigré couple (the Lorentzes) who anxiously await their possessions.[21] Fyodor is moving into the very same pension, accompanied by only a suitcase significantly and revealingly containing "more manuscripts than shirts."[22] He is both observing the scene and consciously filing it in his memory so that later he can recall it to start a novel: "Some day, he thought, I must use such a scene to start a good, thick old-fashioned novel" (*G* 4).

Indeed, that is exactly what he does. When another moving van leaves at the end of the novel, relocating another Russian émigré couple (Zina's parents), Fyodor thinks back to the very first moving scene while formulating to Zina his future work: "'Here is what I'd like to do,' he said. 'Something similar to destiny's work in regard to us. Think how fate started it three and a half odd years ago. . . . The first attempt to bring us together was crude and heavy! That moving of furniture, for example: I see something extravagant in it, a "no-holds-barred" something, for it was quite a job moving the Lorentzes and all their belongings into the house where I had just rented a room!'" (363). Within these two moving scenes that frame the action in *The Gift*, we discover several physical relocations undertaken by Fyodor, all coupled with literary thought processes resulting in artistic journeys, or as Toker coins them, "writing exercises."[23] Fyodor resides in three different pensions (this time none is close to the railroad, so now none is shaken continually by passing trains), which correspond to the number of his major literary achievements. It is as if each pension inspires a new style and genre, involves another literary tradition, and initiates a new voice. In the first pension, Fyodor writes his newly published collection of lyrical poetry, which deals with his childhood and is influenced by the poetics of the 1820s. In the next pension, he begins the biography of his father, under the spell of Aleksandr Pushkin. And at the apartment of Zina's parents, he writes his least personal piece, the controversial biography of Chernyshevsky, utilizing the voice of Nikolay Gogol. The three physical relocations across Berlin, coupled with examinations of personal past and explorations of the Russian cultural and literary tradition of the nineteenth century, are journeys that represent a means of finding a voice that will project Fyodor's artistic talent beyond the borders of Russia, journeys allowing him successfully to bridge the two shores—his past and present.[24]

Fyodor's second relocation, to the pension run by a German landlady, Klara Stoboy, presents a move into the protagonist's most personal recollections. Again as in *Mary*, the protagonist's immediate environment is described and symbolically related to his situation. Although not much stress is put on the internal layout of the pension (as was the case in *Mary*), the minimal description presented here is directly linked to Fyodor's passion for writing. Immediately upon entering his new room, he judges its physical appearance—the walls covered by pale yellow wallpaper with bluish tulips, the awaiting empty desk, and the armchair—by its potential to inspire: "It would be hard, he mused, to transform the wallpaper . . . into a distant steppe. . . . And much cigarette ash would have to fall under the armchair and into its folds before it would become suitable for traveling" (*G* 8).[25] Boyd notes the dreariness of this place and sees Fyodor's writing about his past as a way "to escape from the cramped and drab life he is forced to lead . . . to pass through the constricting walls of his room and out to wherever his father might be—the wild spaces of Central Asia, or even paradise itself" (454). I would argue, however, that Fyodor is not mentally trying to escape his rented room or Berlin in general; rather, he is in the process of learning how imaginatively to convert an uninviting and unfamiliar environment into a place of creative activity, into an artistic home that will eventually be transformed into "a distant steppe," a steppe that his father once traversed.

Fyodor's first view of his new room is tied to the vision he has of his future work—the biography of his father. The mention of "much cigarette ash" falling under the armchair, the same armchair to be used for "traveling" (an image that implies participation in his father's travels and, moreover, that writing is a journey as well), suggests both that it will be difficult to make the new lodging suit his artistic needs and that his work will require much time and patience.[26] Indeed, Fyodor's work turns out to be quite complex in its conception. It is presented as a double journey: one inspired by Pushkin, the father of Russian literature, and one inspired by his father, the famous entomologist and traveler who disappeared nine years earlier on his last trip. The reason for "a surge toward Pushkin in Fyodor's literary progress" (*G* foreword) is openly explained in the text: "Continuing his training program during the whole of spring, he fed on Pushkin, inhaled Pushkin (the reader of Pushkin has the capacity of his lungs enlarged). He studied the accuracy of the words and the absolute purity of their conjunction; he carried the transparency of prose to the limits of blank verse and then mastered it" (*G* 97).[27] The desire and need to appropriate the voice of prose and the accuracy of words are described not only as part of Fyodor's artistic growth but also as a physical activity that is time-consuming yet invigorating: Fyodor ends up with "enlarged lungs." The fact that the mastery of the Russian language is occurring in the pension of Klara Stoboy, whose name evokes the Russian language, makes the name less incidental and more likely the result of a playful design or the hand of fate: "Klara Stoboy—which to a Russian's ear sounded with sentimental firmness as Klara is with thee (s toboy)" (*G* 7).[28] Fyodor is not satisfied merely by learning from a master of the literary past. He also reaches into a more intimate past, into the teachings of his father: "'My father,' wrote Fyodor, recalling that time, 'not only taught me a great deal but also trained my very thoughts, as a voice or hand is trained, according to the rules of his school'" (*G* 127).[29] The training of thoughts that Fyodor is referring to is more precisely training in perspicacity (acuteness of sight and keenness of understanding) on the basis of lepidopteral science.[30] And perspicacity is what Fyodor especially needs in exile, in a new territory where his sight and understanding have not yet adapted to the unfamiliar environment, whose inspirational potential he is as of yet unable to detect. In other words, Fyodor needs to learn how to penetrate the bleakness of exile, of his existential situation, so that he can find subject matter to write about. To transcend the problem of becoming silenced by an unknown territory, by the four walls of his pension room, Fyodor needs to sharpen both his vision and his understanding.

Given the importance of perspicacity (Fyodor's father is associated with the ideal form of perspicacity [*N'sO* 118]), it is surprising that the influence of his father's scientific teachings upon Fyodor's literary art—what one might playfully describe as the strengthening of artistic wings with butterfly wings—has escaped the critical attention it deserves.[31] Alexandrov comes closest to discussing the subject, even though he relates it to the otherworld, by noting Nabokov's thoughts about natural science and art:

> In a review of a book on butterflies [Nabokov] asks if "there does not exist a high ridge where the mountainside of 'scientific' knowledge joins the opposite slope of 'artistic' imagination." He answers this rhetorical question in *Speak, Memory* when he postulates that "there is, it would seem, in the dimensional scale of the world a kind

of delicate meeting place between imagination and
knowledge, a point, arrived at by diminishing large things
and enlarging small ones, that is intrinsically artistic."
(*N'sO* 32–33)

These ideas are put into practice especially in chapter 2 of *The
Gift*, in the biography of Fyodor's father. Fyodor links the lepidopteral and the literary, links his own and his father's art, in one
sweeping journey. And he does arrive at a meeting place that is
"intrinsically artistic," for he expands the significance of the
delicate butterflies by connecting them to art while reducing the
potentially extensive discussions about art to a few lessons about
butterflies. In other words, he pins down butterflies for observation, but he also relates these observations to the art of writing
in general, to the pursuit of his own voice. More specifically, the
lessons about the order Lepidoptera that are recalled by Fyodor
are twofold: how to find art and how to understand it. The first
has to do with deliberately seeking out the unexpected, training
eyesight so that it can capture the artistic in nature; the second
relates to mimicry, through reading, elucidating, and explaining.
These two lessons expand the art of perception and have a direct influence on Fyodor's future literary development. These
two lessons turn out to be the key to artistic success in exile.

As discussed above in section one, the idea of the unexpected
is already introduced in *Mary*. The sudden discovery of a long-
lost loved one, through a photograph located in a desk drawer
of a Russian pension in Berlin, in the least predicted of places,
has the power to bring forth a highly creative and imaginative
journey into the past, a journey crucial to personal success in
exile. Since the protagonist of *Mary* is not a writer, the idea of
the unexpected as inspirational is only cursorily alluded to or
made relevant to art. Nor is the unexpected deliberately sought
out. In *The Gift*, however, Fyodor, as an artist, learns to realize
that the unexpected needs to be consciously sought out, that it
is a crucial part of the artistic process, of his growth as a writer,
that it contains mystery and inspiration. Thus Fyodor recalls his
father's Lepidoptera lessons that pertain to the unexpected. His
first example is the memory of his father's "special smile" (*G* 109)
when he points out that the Black Ringlet butterfly appears "with
mysterious and elegant unexpectedness" (109) only in even years.[32]
The father's smile symbolizes the special joy associated with a

unique discovery. The second memory about the unexpected is connected to the Blue butterfly (*Maculinea arion* [Lycaenidae]).[33]

> He taught me how to take apart an ant-hill and find the caterpillar of a Blue which had concluded a barbaric pact with its inhabitants, and I saw how an ant, greedily tickling a hind segment of that caterpillar's clumsy, sluglike little body, forced it to excrete a drop of intoxicant juice, which it swallowed immediately. In compensation it offered its own larvae as food; it was as if cows gave us Chartreuse and we gave them our infants to eat. But the strong caterpillar of one exotic species of Blue will not stoop to this exchange, brazenly devouring the infant ants and then turning into an impenetrable chrysalis which finally, at the time of hatching, is surrounded by ants (those failures in the school of experience) awaiting the emergence of the helplessly crumpled butterfly in order to attack it; they attack—and nevertheless she does not perish: "I have never laughed so much," said my father, "as when I realized that nature had supplied her with a sticky substance which caused the feelers and feet of those zealous ants to get stuck together, so that they rolled and writhed all around her while she herself, calm and invulnerable, let her wings strengthen and dry." (*G* 110)[34]

The approach to the unexpected is presented in this lesson as a series of steps. The first step is realizing that it surrounds us everywhere, even in the seemingly mundane anthill. The second step is in the uncovering of protective layers that prevent one from direct observation, the looking beneath the surface, taking something apart so that at the end the symbiotic relationship between the ant and the caterpillar is revealed. The third step is cultivating the patience necessary to discover the truly unexpected phenomenon, which turns out to be not the relationship between the ants and the caterpillar but what happens when the butterfly begins to unfold from its chrysalis, calmly tricking the ants with its stickiness. The implied patience required to observe this deceptive and protective mechanism of the Blue is reflected stylistically through the use of one long, convoluted, and laborious sentence that in turn requires the reader's patience. As Boyd notes about Fyodor's style, in general, "Almost every long sinuous sentence bulges with parentheses, like a snake rendered sluggish after swallowing too many plump, irresistible mice. Sentences stretch to accommodate their ample prey, the unruliness and the stray beauty of an inexhaustible world" (452). However, such sentences can become convoluted, and advancement (swallowing) can become difficult. The story, the protagonist, and the reader seem to be getting nowhere. Yet, despite this, Boyd assures, "In accord with the novel's pattern, even crueler frustrations turn into the most unexpected rewards" (452). And indeed, in the case of this observation, the end result is unexpected, for the butterfly beautifully deceives the ants, thus allowing the metamorphosis to be successfully completed. At this point, the father's patience and sharp observation skills are amply rewarded: "I have never laughed so much." This laughter reveals the joy of solving and understanding something mysterious and unexpected, something that few are privilege to, for it is hidden from casual glance.

The reason Fyodor recalls this particular lesson from among all others is that metaphorically it characterizes his present existential situation.[35] He is like a larva—the developing offspring of his sweeping, majestic butterfly father—still trapped within his unmetamorphosed state until he finds the wings of his gift, his art. However, unlike most butterflies, whose chrysalises can undergo metamorphosis in a familiar environment, be it an anthill or the branch of a tree, Fyodor is in a foreign and unknown environment of exile, where he still has to figure out how successfully to unfurl his wings without being eaten by the zealous ants. In other words, he needs to figure out how to expand and develop his artistic voice so that it will not become silenced by his surroundings. He is searching for his own particular substance to survive. This substance need not be sticky; another species of the Blue butterfly produces tiny violinlike particles (their shape evokes the artist's voice), which the ants devour instead of the butterfly itself.[36] But, as Fyodor realizes from his father's lesson, it must be unexpectedly imaginative, mysteriously deceptive, and ultimately rewarding.

This awareness is displayed in Fyodor's subsequent writing exercise, the biography of Chernyshevsky, where he follows, or mimics, his father's lepidopteral teachings. He pursues the unexpected, the subject "about the great man of the sixties" (*G* 40), the very subject he so vehemently refused when it was offered to him (before he even began to write his father's biography) by

Chernyshevsky's namesake, a fellow émigré, Chernyshevsky. At that prior time, such an excursion into the life of a civic critic seemed too foreign, uninteresting, and uninspiring, even in his recollection of Rozanov's words: "a syringe of sulphuric acid" (173). However, not long after abandoning the biography of his father, he stumbles upon a Soviet chess magazine, which features the article "Chernyshevski and Chess." The encounter results not in a heightened interest in chess problems but in an unexpected stab from the muse, symbolized by a smile and by a curiosity precisely about the once-dismissed subject—now provoked by "the two-column extract from Chernyshevski's youthful diary" (194). Fyodor's smile, of course, brings to mind his father's smile associated with the mysterious and unexpected behavior of the Black Ringlet butterfly—its even-year appearance. Thus the smile links not only father and son but also the natural sciences and humanities. The lesson learned from natural science is now pursued by the writer, Fyodor, who realizes that the subject needs further dissection; he proceeds to the state library, where he borrows the complete works of Chernyshevsky: "And as he read, his astonishment grew, and this feeling contained a peculiar kind of bliss" (195). As Chernyshevsky slowly begins to unfold from his chrysalis, Fyodor realizes that the life of this man is full of unexpected turns and rewards. It teaches him about another's experience of exile, about personal heroism, and it provides him with richness (imagery and subject matter) that would delight any creator. Furthermore, through the prism of Chernyshevsky's life, Fyodor gains a better understanding of his own situation in exile. It is as if Fyodor has got hold of a kaleidoscope that projects both what is outside (fragments of Chernyshevsky's life) and what is inside (fragments of Fyodor's life). (I return to Chernyshevsky and his relevance to Fyodor in chapter 3.)

The lesson about the unexpected is followed directly by one concerning mimicry, which is equally important to Fyodor's writing. It is a lesson in how to view the world in a way that extends beyond utilitarian purposes, beyond the mimetic. The father, while explaining to his son the basic principles of mimicry, is quick to point out that the preservative function alone cannot explain the exquisitely intricate patterns these butterflies have:

> He told me about the incredible artistic wit of mimetic disguise, which was not explainable by the struggle for

existence (the rough haste of evolution's unskilled forces), was too refined for the mere deceiving of accidental predators, feathered, scaled and otherwise (not very fastidious, but then not too fond of butterflies), and seemed to have been invented by some waggish artist precisely for the intelligent eyes of man (a hypothesis that may lead far an evolutionist who observes apes feeding on butterflies); he told me about these magic masks of mimicry; about the enormous moth which in a state of repose assumes the image of a snake looking at you. (110)

Here the father not only points out the inadequacy of utilitarian or evolutionary principles but also stresses the importance of possessing "intelligent eyes."[37] Only to those who have such eyes will the lepidopteral artistry be revealed. For butterflies have the ability to deceive their predators, as well as those whose vision is not opened or accustomed to the magical and unexpected. Much later in the novel, Fyodor relates to Zina that "the most enchanting things in nature and art are based on deception" (*G* 364), but to discover this one must first be aware that the deception exists, must be able to see or read the world through "intelligent eyes."

At the beginning of *The Gift*, Fyodor is vulnerable, easily deceived in his new environment, for his eyesight is not yet accustomed to his surroundings, as is demonstrated in the tram scene. While going to a language lesson that he has no desire to conduct, Fyodor ponders the people around him, the alien Germans. They evoke a feeling in him "unworthy of an artist" (81), one of irritation and fury. Looking at the back of one man in particular, he indulges in a lengthy and biased indictment. Yet this supposed German unexpectedly turns out to be a compatriot, taking out of his pocket a copy of an émigré Russian newspaper. Fyodor's reaction to the mistaken identity is worth noting: "That's wonderful, thought Fyodor, almost smiling with delight. How clever, how gracefully sly and how essentially good life is! Now he made out in the newspaper reader's features such a compatriotic softness—in the corners of the eyes, large nostrils, a Russian-cut mustache—that it became at once both funny and incomprehensible how anyone could have been deceived. His thoughts were cheered by this unexpected respite and had already taken a different turn" (82). As Fyodor's eyes gain a more sharpened focus, he realizes that he was deceived not so much by the back of this particular Russian—which indeed may look exactly like, may mimic, the back of any German—as by his own sight. He is guilty of a lack of careful observation, of tripping over his own hasty conclusion. Yet once Fyodor discovers his mistake, he realizes that he is lucky after all to have had such an experience, that his path is littered with precious visual moments worthy of an artist. As already discussed, a smile can indicate a moment of realization, inspiration, discovery, and here Fyodor too smiles at "how gracefully sly and how essentially good life is" even in exile, in Berlin.

Heeding his father's lesson, Fyodor appropriates "the magic masks of mimicry," the artistically intricate butterfly pattern, for his following work, the biography of Chernyshevsky. Fyodor pins down Chernyshevsky in such a way that the topic transcends his numerous original intentions for taking on the project: to gain a distance from his personal past, to have a "firing practice" (196), to cheer up his émigré friend Chernyshevsky, and to approach a subject that "represents everything that Fyodor is not."[38] All these reasons are explicitly stated or become obvious throughout the reading. However, the initially utilitarian pattern of the biography can no longer be explained when Fyodor weaves into it an artistry and structural patterning that is reserved for only him and the "intelligent eyes" of the reader. In a sense, Fyodor retaliates against Chernyshevsky's belief that reality (even when seen through half-blinded eyes) is better than art.

The two lessons of perspicacity—the importance of the unexpected and the beauty of mimicry—recalled and described in the biography of Fyodor's father become successfully implemented in Fyodor's future biography of Chernyshevsky. However, while trying to write about his father, Fyodor loses both control over his sight and power over his subject. As Connolly puts it, he "loses that critical measure of detachment which the writer requires when giving completion to the inner life of another, and he in effect displaces the other with a projection of his own interiority" (202). Thus Fyodor's attempts to use fiction to represent his father's life fail as the imaginative bridge collapses—he gets sucked into the abyss of becoming what he writes about, cannot (yet) sustain a self against the seductive lure of the past. Again in Connolly's words, "The most satisfying art occupies a middle ground, and Fyodor's quest for the correct balance needs further refinement" (204). Fyodor abandons the biography because he realizes that he has lost the ability to retain a contrapuntal vision. And although he has pinned down his subject, he has not fully described it; he has instead described himself. He needs not only to appropriate his personal past but also to step out of it so that it will guide his present.[39] As the biography comes to an end for Fyodor, both because he is dissatisfied with it and because he is displaced from his pension, the wallpaper comes into focus again: "I lived here exactly two years, thought here about many things, the shadows of my caravan passed over this wallpaper, lilies grew out of the cigarette ash on the carpet, but now the journey is over" (*G* 144). The unexpected has happened after all in this room. The bleakest of environments has produced art and broadened artistic vision. Yet more is needed, the power of critical distance, and that in itself is another of Fyodor's discoveries.

We can compare the process of writing his father's biography to an event related to lepidopterology that Fyodor remembers witnessing as a young boy. His father had just returned from his travels, bringing back an undescribed moth species, *Epicnaptera arborea* (Lasiocampidae). Yet on the first day on his walk around the estate "with no thought to Lepidoptera" (95), he came upon the very same moth, in an environment that had been well investigated: "But the momentum of mighty coincidence did not stop there, it was good for one more stage: only a few days later his father learned that this new moth had just been described from St. Petersburg specimens by a fellow scientist, and Fyodor cried all night long: they had beaten Father to it!" (95). There was no need to travel so far to gain the special moth. But Fyodor did not understand then, as his father did, that the journey itself sometimes can be more important than whatever is physically brought back. The *Epicnaptera arborea* "reflects in its name the epic quality of the father's life," which stresses the importance of the journey itself.[40] For Fyodor, the biography of his father results in the same type of journey. The butterfly (his father) is not successfully described by him, but the journey itself (the writing process) yields results. Through the search for his father's essence by way of personal memory, Fyodor has defined a clearer vision of what art should be and where his own weaknesses lie.

The remembered lesson about the painstaking observation of the Blue butterfly is more than just a lesson in perspicacity, more than just a lesson in how to locate the unexpected, the artistic, in the unfamiliar territory of exile. It also comes to serve as a structural model for Fyodor's biography of his father.

In writing the biography, Fyodor moves from the least creative approach, a mere copying of other sources, to the most imaginative in a way that mirrors the approach needed to depart from the seemingly mundane (the anthill) to arrive at the unexpected concealed within (the chrysalis's successful transformation into a butterfly). Fyodor begins the project with a general presentation of his father's life by copying an account out of an encyclopedia. Here the narrative voice takes on the objective, dry tone of a reference book entry, with all information presented in brisk and skeletal fashion: "Between 1885 and 1918 he covered an incredible amount of territory, making surveys of his route on a three-mile scale for a distance of many thousands of miles and forming astounding collections" (*G* 103).[41] Thus, in a page and a half, "the general scheme" (*G* 103) of the father's life is given in a kind of outline form. Then Fyodor, as well as the novel, presents a segment of a letter from his mother in which she relates a few private memories of her husband and his passion for Lepidoptera. This letter obviously provides a bit more personal information than the encyclopedia does, yet rather than creatively incorporate the information it provides into his own narrative, Fyodor merely copies it too. In a sense, the letter and the encyclopedia entry can be seen as the outside layers of the biography, providing, for the most part, only basic information about Fyodor's father; this outside information also reveals very little about the author of the biography, since Fyodor attained it through research and copying rather than through any kind of artistic process.

After this uncreative and minimally personal recount, Fyodor finally plunges into a deeper level of exposure, into his own writing based on personal recollections. This narrative is made up of memory fragments, which provide an insider's view into the aspects of the father's life that are centered around lepidopterology. We are presented with the description of the father's study and individual captures, his acute observations during a walk with Fyodor, his voice when he talked about his favorite subject, his special smile accompanying a discovery, and his behavior toward natives of Tibet, family members, and especially Fyodor. These bits and pieces of the past follow each other in random fashion, mirroring the random flow of memories. And because these memories are presented as separate entities, not linked together by smooth transitions or a linear narrative line, they stand out as highly evocative and impressionistic. It is as if the reader is allowed to have a look into a box full of precious photographs from the past. Fyodor, however, is not satisfied with this personal account, for he is still unable to convey the most important and mysterious of his father's personal traits: "an enigmatic reserve" and "an aura of something still unknown but which was perhaps the most genuine of all" (*G* 114).[42]

Fyodor begins to seek this "aura of something still unknown"—the innermost layer or center of the biography—by embarking on a description of his father's entomological journey to Tibet. However, because Fyodor was never allowed to accompany his father on any of his travels, Fyodor's general attempt to recount memories is superseded here by a highly fictionalized and imaginative account. It is as if Fyodor has borrowed artistic wings from one of the butterflies accompanying his father, and he re-creates this journey from the perspective of an active participant. He comments on the makeup of their caravan, the traversed scenery, their mutual discovery of an unknown species of snake with an undescribed mouse in its stomach, and so on. However, in the course of this imaginative narrative, Fyodor places himself in such close proximity to his father that Fyodor suddenly becomes indistinguishable from the great lepidopterist and explorer. This blurring is especially apparent on the stylistic level. The first-person singular narration—"I see him leaning down from the saddle amid a clatter of sliding stones" (*G* 117)—abruptly switches to the first-person plural—"Spring awaited us in the mountains of Nan-Shan" (120).[43] In other words, father and son have merged. This union consequently displaces the father from his central position in the biography. Recalling that Fyodor's original goal in the imaginative section was to discover his father's "aura of something still unknown," we realize that this aim can no longer be achieved because of the disappearance of the central subject himself, the absorption of the father into the "we" of Fyodor's imagination.

When Fyodor realizes his failure, he snaps out of his imaginary journey to Tibet by suddenly focusing on his prosaic Berlin reality—"the dead and impossible tulips of his wallpaper, the crumbling mound of cigarette butts in the ashtray, and the lamp's reflection in the black windowpane" (*G* 125). However, the writer's return to the present tense, to his desk, is brief, lasting only a paragraph. The next paragraph begins with the sentence "He remembered with incredible vividness, as if he had preserved that sunny day in a velvet case" (125), a sentence that immediately takes us back to the past world of Fyodor's memories. We can interpret this brisk temporal move, from imaginative fiction to Berlin and then back to memory, as Fyodor's climb away from the biography's unreached center (the mystery of the father) up through the same layers as those he had worked through to move closer to the center. (A copied letter from his mother expressing her belief that Fyodor would one day write this book makes up the last layer of the ascent.)

The structure of the above outline of Fyodor's work in its progression from the outermost to the innermost layer, from the mimetic to the most imaginative, exhibits the same approach as that used in the dismantling of the anthill of the Blue butterfly. Like the anthill's mundane appearance on the surface, providing the typical scenery of ants at work, the encyclopedia entry and the recopied letter from Fyodor's mother give us only skeletal information about the life of Godunov-Cherdyntsev Sr. The more Fyodor is submerged in his own memories, in recollections of the lessons learned from his father, the more understanding he gains about the natural sciences and artistic vision. This understanding in turn brings him even closer to his subject, both to his father and to his writing project. It is precisely at this point, so close to the center of discovery—the chrysalis's secret defense mechanism (the sticky substance) or the father's "aura of something still unknown" (the aloofness)—that the peeling of layers requires further perseverance, keen understanding, creativity, imagination, and ultimately precise observational skills.[44] Here Fyodor makes his mistake by too forcefully moving in one direction, solely relying on his imagination. The biography turns into fiction. In other words, as the writer indicates to his mother in a letter, he has contaminated his work with "a kind of secondary poetization, which keeps departing further and further from that real poetry with which the lived experience of these receptive, knowledgeable and chaste naturalists endowed their research" (*G* 139).[45] Now he understands that a careful balance of memories of the past and creative imagination is necessary to arrive best at his artistic goals. Since he was unable to achieve that balance, he abandons the project.[46] If I may use a butterfly image as Nabokov so often does, the biography does not emerge from Fyodor's room with its wings spread out displaying artistic patterns. Instead, it lies dormant in Fyodor's room in the form of a "swarm of drafts, long manuscript extracts from books, indecipherable jottings on miscellaneous sheets of papers" (*G* 138). In other words, it is still shapeless, chaotic.

Fyodor's structural approach, which, in terms of the biography, we could describe as the peeling of layers to arrive at the core of things, is a micropresentation of his overall artistic development depicted in the novel as a whole. *The Gift* is a *Künstlerroman* in which Fyodor moves from one layer of artistic development to another, from a writer of lyric poetry to an author of epic biography to a more direct encounter with ironic realism and, finally, to the author of the novel *The Gift*.[47] As already stated in the previous section, the poetry about his childhood, the biography of his father, and Chernyshevsky's biography constitute the main layers of Fyodor's artistic development.[48] It is not the move from one genre to another, from one voice to another, that is of interest here but rather how these works are positioned in relation to each other in the overall structure of the novel.

To understand the complex interconnections between Fyodor's various literary endeavors, we might think of his development as forming a spiral.[49] The poetry collection constitutes the first loop of the spiral, which leads into the biography of Fyodor's father, forming the second loop, which in turn leads into the third loop, the cultural biography of Chernyshevsky. The spiral image is much more appropriate for visualizing the complex way these narrative pieces interlock than, for instance, the image of a ladder, because stylistically Fyodor's individual works are all neatly framed, thus forming a loop. For example, his poetry collection begins with "Lost Ball" and ends with "Found Ball"; the biography of Fyodor's father begins and ends with fragments of his mother's letters; and Chernyshevsky's biography is framed by inverted parts of a sonnet. These literary endeavors, although in separate chapters, are not self-contained but evolve one from the other; each one leads into the next, thus forming a spiral (implying artistic progression) rather than a series of independent circles.[50]

The pattern of an encircling framework is in fact evident in the entire novel, which is itself framed by moving scenes appearing on the first and last pages. Furthermore, as Boyd points out, the last page of *The Gift* ends with Pushkinian lines, which invite the reader to return to the beginning:

> As he evokes the end of *Eugene Onegin,* Fyodor sends us back to his arrival at Tannenberg Street, fate's first push toward Zina, and describes that scene in terms that evoke the beginning of *Dead Souls.* No lover of Russian literature could fail to know that it was Pushkin who gave Gogol the idea for *Dead Souls*—as Fyodor's strangely Pushkinian father seems to have prompted both Fyodor's first move toward Zina and toward the novel that now commemorates that first prompting of kindly fate. (*VN:RY* 473–74)

By combining this idea of the external frame of the novel's beginning and end with the idea that each of Fyodor's major literary endeavors forms one loop of a spiral, we can imagine a spiral within one overriding frame, or within a circle. Philip Sicker points out that Nabokov describes his own life in similar terms: "His tools were memory and art, and through their related agency he sought to unify the constituent parts of his ego, to trace the 'colored spiral in a small ball of glass' that was the pattern of his life."[51] This image is useful in trying to visualize the complex structure of *The Gift.* The spiral is made of three rotations, representing the three creative works by Fyodor. Significantly, the central rotation is the biography of Fyodor's father. It is this center that reveals the structure of the entire novel, for the dismantling of the Blue butterfly's anthill suggests the entire structure of *The Gift* with its many framed layers. Then the entire spiral is within the glass ball which is *The Gift,* the novel form. A reader progresses along each loop, journeying along the spiral and then arriving at the surface of the ball, which prompts the realization that, as the reader finishes the novel, he or she is propelled back to its beginning, realizing that the very narrative he or she has just completed is what Fyodor talks about as his intended work.

This elaborate structure mirrors the extraordinary artistic development Fyodor achieves by the end of the novel. Fyodor succeeds in exile by finding a literary voice that encompasses or reveals a holistic vision, one that incorporates various kinds of discourses (from the encyclopedic to the lyrical), genres (from poetry to prose), and experiences (from his tutoring in the gray dreariness of Berlin to the memories of his father's Lepidoptera lessons). The structure of the novel too mirrors this all-encompassing vision; the fragments of the narrative are not isolated pieces somehow encircled at the outermost edge by a frame but are carefully interlocking pieces that, if viewed in this complete totality, come together in a startling, unexpected pattern, like the beautiful surprise in the turn of a kaleidoscope.

In *Mary* and *The Gift*, personal memories are evoked through butterflies, photographs, wallpaper designs, letters, and flashes from childhood. Scattered throughout the novels, these objects seem at first haphazardly placed here and there, with no higher pattern in mind. Yet through one's power of memory, imagination, artistic selection, blending, and repositioning, these snippets complete a picture, a story. In Nabokov's world, stories that are woven out of memories have great powers: they grant physical and mental recuperation, they impart perspicacity and meaning. Yet it is not always so, as will be seen in the following chapter, in which Kundera's presentation of memory looms darkly.

2. Milan Kundera:
Variations on Letters and Bowler Hats

Tamina—about whom the narrator of *The Book of Laughter and Forgetting* (1979) says, "It is a novel about Tamina, and whenever Tamina is absent, it is a novel for Tamina"—is one of the most heart-wrenching heroines in all of Kundera's fiction.[1] Struggling to connect a bleak present with the recuperative fragments of the past, Tamina first tries to reconstruct her past life by writing down dates and places of its events. Later, her fear of continual forgetting leads to desperate attempts to retrieve eleven notebooks, left behind in Prague, that document her life before exile. When she fails and the diaries remain locked in a desk drawer behind the iron curtain, death soon follows for Tamina; she winds up trapped on a strange island inhabited solely by children, where no past or memories exist. Her story, although it appears deceptively simple, is integral to the entire narrative of *The Book of Laughter and Forgetting*. The story of Tamina, especially because of her failure, dramatizes the importance of sustaining personal memory through imaginative links to the past.

Tamina's ultimate failure to sustain imaginative connections is most clearly represented through her inability to re-create or retrieve her lost notebooks. At first, when Tamina is still in Czechoslovakia, her husband, who is ten years older than she and thus has "some idea of how poor the human memory can be" (*BLF* 84), encourages her to keep a diary of their shared life. She complies, despite regarding this writing exercise as a mundane chore. The many empty pages and the overall fragmentary nature of her entries reveal Tamina's lack of interest and creativity. She is capable of only a literal transcription of the "days of dissatisfaction, quarrels, even boredom" (86).[2]

However, Tamina's husband dies shortly after their emigration, and once she is alone in exile, the diaries left behind in a desk drawer at her mother-in-law's house become increasingly important.[3] They become her only means of recovering the past, the life she shared with her husband in Czechoslovakia. Since Tamina, as a political émigré, is unable to retrieve the diaries herself, she first tries to rewrite them: "Her project, like Don Quixote's, is predicated on an ingenuous belief that words and images in the mind possess the power to resurrect the past."[4] Driven by the prospect of mimetically re-creating the past, she buys a new notebook and divides it into eleven parts, one part for each of the lost years of her life. But because in exile Tamina shares her past with no one with whom to double-check a forgotten event or date, and because she is unable to revisit the specific physical places that might help her recall events, she has a difficult time re-creating the precise details of her life. Devastated because she has "lost all sense of chronology" (*BLF* 85), as well as any sense of location, and is thus unable to transcribe the exact dates and vacation spots of all eleven years, Tamina gives up on the project. It is this obsession with specific details that prevents her from re-creating the past more spontaneously, imaginatively, and freely, which ultimately prevents her from re-creating it at all.

Finally, Tamina decides that the only other means of regaining her personal past is by reclaiming the original notebooks. She asks her Western acquaintances to go to Prague and pick up the diaries at her mother-in-law's house. Thus, through these acquaintances, Tamina is trying to build an artificial bridge between the two countries, a bridge that would allow her past to be carried over onto the new shore. Significantly, she never tells these acquaintances the true contents of the diaries. Tamina's silence on this issue is tied to the protection of her identity, for she feels that, if her private life were to be made public, she would be stripped of her identity.

> She realized that what gave her written memories value, meaning, was that they were meant for *her alone*. As soon as they lost that quality, the intimate chain binding her to them would be broken, and instead of reading them with her own eyes, she would be forced to read them from the point of view of an audience perusing an impersonal document. Then the woman who wrote them would lose her identity, and the striking similarity that would nonetheless remain between her and the author of the notes would be nothing but a parody, a mockery. (100–101)

It is not only the alteration of Tamina's eyes—reading her life from an outsider's perspective—that is at stake here. Tamina is also worried about the eyes of others; she compares them to "rain washing away inscriptions on a stone wall. Or light ruining a print by hitting photographic paper before it goes into the developer" (100). In essence, she believes that these eyes have the power to destroy or erase the contents of her diaries, which now represent not just her identity but her entire life. Tamina knows that there is no need to worry about the prying curiosity of her acquaintances because they are too self-absorbed to ask any questions. She is, however, justifiably concerned with the interrogative gaze of the Czech secret police, who read all correspondence with foreign countries, and that is why she never has her mother-in-law mail the diaries. At the end, ironically, it is the very mother-in-law entrusted with these documents whose curiosity desecrates Tamina's private world.[5]

The other motivation for Tamina's silence about what it is that she so desperately wants to retrieve is a cultural difference she encounters in the West. She feels that here privacy is not as sacred as it was behind the iron curtain, where people had nothing left but their few private moments, and even private moments were constantly jeopardized by the ever-present secret police. Explaining to her acquaintances why she needs to keep her personal life private would prove difficult, if not impossible, because here people, as if to mock privacy, voluntarily give up their most intimate moments. This cultural difference becomes especially evident when Tamina and her acquaintances watch television together.

> "The first time I had sex I was fifteen"—the round old head looked proudly from one panel member to the next—"that's right, fifteen. I am now sixty-five. That means a sex life of fifty years' duration. Assuming I have made love on the average of twice a week—a very modest estimate—that means a hundred times a year or five thousand times so far. Let's go on. If an orgasm lasts five seconds, I have twenty-five thousand seconds of orgasm to my credit. Which comes to a total of six hours and fifty-six minutes. Not bad, eh?" (*BLF* 97)

Unlike her acquaintances, who take the old man's bragging seriously, Tamina bursts out laughing, envisioning a continuous orgasm that makes the old man first lose his false teeth and then suffer a heart attack. His imagined death is grotesque, as well as revealing. To Tamina, the reduction of a life to a single act repeated without pause—an act that has been stripped of privacy, past, meaning, and context—is not glorious but deadly.

However, it is not only the cultural difference based on the importance of privacy that prevents Tamina from ever discussing her personal past. It is also her overall unwillingness to bridge the two cultures herself, for she realizes that it would be impossible to explain her previous life to nonémigrés in a way that would preserve and honor its richness and complexity: "Tamina had long since realized that if she wanted to make her life comprehensible to people here she had to simplify it. It would have been impossibly complicated to explain why private letters and diaries might be confiscated and why she set such great store by them" (94). So Tamina allows these go-betweens to believe that the diaries are political documents, for as such their importance would seemingly be obvious and understandable. The narrator reflects Tamina's inability ever to explain fully her native country's historical reality by creating a textual gap precisely at the one moment she is "making a long and impassioned speech" (95) about the situation in Czechoslovakia to Hugo, one of the potential retrievers of her diaries. The content of this long, impassioned speech, especially significant because it is the only speech that Tamina makes about her country, is not only missing, unnarrated, but the omission is emphasized by the narrator's following comment on the veracity of Tamina's words: "She knew the country inside out, and I can tell you—everything she said was true" (95). The narrator's emphasis on the truth of Tamina's speech ironically calls attention to its inaccessibility to the reader. The narrator is reflecting Tamina's cultural difficulty on the structural level of the text here, but perhaps he is also suggesting that to bridge a cultural gap that separates an émigré from a nonémigré is nearly impossible.[6]

When Tamina realizes that her diaries will never be retrieved (her last prospect ends with Hugo, who out of sexual and emotional frustration is unwilling to undertake the trip to Czechoslovakia), she collapses into a blurred and faded existence, into an abyss. No longer responsive to her customers, no longer lending them her ear, and no longer participating in their conversations, she alienates herself from the lives of those around her through silence. In essence, Tamina voluntarily chooses to exacerbate her outer, physical exile with an inner one. The double exile naturally results in a reductive existence. From now on, Tamina only silently and mechanically serves coffee, nevermore inquiring about her surroundings, nevermore phoning back home to ask about the diaries. The first section to deal with Tamina's story comes to a cold and simple narrative end: "She went on serving coffee and never made another call to Czechoslovakia" (*BLF* 115).

Tamina's silenced present existence is reflected in the structural layout of the narrative, for her story is interrupted immediately following the line about her mechanically serving coffee. The narrator abruptly abandons the narrative thread of Tamina's story and begins a new part, which introduces other characters and issues. Part 2 presents the story of unfulfilled love between a butcher's wife, Kristýna, and a poet-student who spends an evening of debauchery with many famous Czech poets, a story that includes a discussion of the Czech word *litost,* which according to the narrator does not translate exactly into any other language. The narrator, in fact, takes the time to explain that *litost* is an open word denoting many different meanings all fused together: "It designates a feeling as infinite as an open accordion, a feeling that is the synthesis of many others: grief, sympathy, remorse, and an indefinable longing. The first syllable, which is long and stressed, sounds like the wail of an abandoned dog" (121). The untranslatability of this word creates an epistemological gap within the text. In essence, translators are warned that they cannot do justice in translating this word and that the Czech original will always denote more than the translation. This linguistic gap mirrors the inherent cultural gap implied in Tamina's section.

Not until part 6, some forty pages later, does the narrator finally return to Tamina. This gap in the story line represents the narrator's own temporary exile of Tamina, as if to reflect her self-imposed exile, as if to honor her desire for silence. The double treatment of her story, in two distinct sections of the narrative (parts 4 and 6), also structurally mirrors the heroine's own doubly exiled existence (inner and outer).[7]

The narrator's return to Tamina begins with the pronouncement that she simply disappeared one day (as she had from the text), explaining that the local police placed her name in the file of "Permanently Missing," "a bureaucratic category easily applied to the dead or exiled."[8] Only then are we given a more detailed account of her disappearance. One day a young man in jeans walks into the café where Tamina works, and he strikes up a conversation. The reason Tamina breaks her silence and responds to this man is that he differs from all the others; he does not speak about himself but instead directs his fast-paced sentences at her. He encourages her, "Forget your forgetting," as he reveals to Tamina, "what she calls remembering is in fact something different, that in fact she is under a spell and watching herself forget" (*BLF* 163). In the original, as pointed out by Maria Němcová Banerjee, the conversion of remembering to forgetting is underscored by a common verbal root that the words share—*vzpomínání* (the act of remembering) and *zapomínání* (the act of forgetting)—thus "remembrance turns into forgetting with a simple flip of a prefix *(za-* instead of *vz-)*" (*TP* 175–76). Furthermore, the man offers Tamina the classic vacation line—"Haven't you ever felt like getting away from it all?"—describing the place to which he can take her as a place "where things are as light as the breeze, where things have no weight" (*BLF* 164). Tamina agrees to ride off in a red sports car with this young man, whose name, Raphael, is "not the least bit accidental" (166).

The critic Fred Misurella takes up the narrator's hint and explores just how Raphael's name is more than accidental by reflecting on the angel Raphael in the Book of Tobit, a story found in the Apocrypha.[9] The biblical story is indeed of interest here, for it contains parallels to Tamina's story in its concern with exiles and a journey guided by an angel, Raphael, to retrieve something from the past. The story is as follows:

> The ostensible setting of the story is the Assyrian capital, Nineveh, where the people of Northern Israel had been taken captive in the latter part of the eighth century B.C. (2 Kg. 17.1–6). There, it is said, dwelt the pious Tobit, who, despite his many charitable deeds, became blind and poor (chs. 1–2). But God heard his prayer, as well as the prayer of demon-haunted Sarah in faraway Media, and sent the angel Raphael to save them both (ch. 3). When Tobit commissioned his son Tobias to collect a deposit of money he had made long before in Media, the angel accompanied him and revealed magic formulas which would heal his father's blindness and exorcise Sarah's demon-lover, As-

modeus (chs. 4–6). Tobias successfully completed his mission and married Sarah (chs. 7–14).[10]

In the biblical story, Raphael is an invaluable angelic intercessor who, with his magical powers, fulfills prayers and protects against evil. Tamina's Raphael, on the other hand, although he does act as a guide who helps to retrieve a moment from her past, ultimately proves to be far different from the helpful biblical guide. As elsewhere in *The Book of Laughter and Forgetting,* this angel is instead a frightening representative of a lifestyle that promotes the dangerous laughter of forgetting, which ends in death.[11]

Tamina understands the danger of what Raphael represents and offers only after it is too late to resist the seductive lure of forgetting. When Raphael stops the car and they stand at the top of a clay slope with an abandoned bulldozer nearby, she suddenly experiences a strong sense of déjà vu, a feeling that the landscape looks "exactly like the terrain around where her husband worked in Czechoslovakia" (*BLF* 166). She remembers the anguished love of their long-ago Sunday walks together, made more poignant because her husband had been fired from his original job and had become a bulldozer operator, and she could get from Prague to see him only once a week. She is overwhelmed by a sense of despair similar to what she felt then and is "glad for the lost fragment of the past [that the landscape] had unexpectedly returned to her" (166). For a brief moment, the two worlds have metaphorically merged for Tamina; she has created a bridge between the two shores. Therefore, feeling that her husband remains alive in her grief, just as all memories remain alive in the emotions of those still living, she begins to regret her decision to accompany Raphael. The narrative moves into exclamatory, free, indirect discourse to emphasize the importance of Tamina's epiphany: "No, no, her husband was still alive in her grief, just lost that's all, and it was her job to look for him! Search the whole world over! Yes, yes! Now she understood. Finally! We will never remember anything by sitting in one place waiting for the memories to come back to us of their own accord! Memories are scattered all over the world. We must travel if we want to find them and flush them from their hiding places!" (167). Although Tamina's thoughts are powerful and passionate, they are never expressed aloud. On the outside, she remains passive; as if to confirm this passivity, she obediently joins Raphael's infectious laughter, a laughter that promises to erase her misery, a laughter that signals forgetting. And now Raphael truly becomes the messenger of forgetting when he grabs Tamina by the arm and both slide down the slippery slope of the clay bank, a "concrete" portrayal of the slide down the figurative slippery slope of no return.[12] At the edge of the water is a rowboat ready with a boy who will become Tamina's new guide. Tamina's journey is increasingly turning into an allegorical one, and as noted by Misurella, "It's hard not to see this water as mythical—as the Lethe, for instance, the river of forgetfulness in Greek mythology, or the Acheron, the river Dante has dividing the borderland of Hell from Limbo" (39–40). From here Tamina is taken to the hauntingly perverse island of children, an island without past, without memory, without individual distinctions.

Just as the salesman Gregor Samsa of Kafka's *Metamorphosis,* whose transformation into a large insect during a night of bad dreams, has been interpreted as a literalization of his passive acceptance of humiliation and drudgery in his day-to-day life, Tamina too, we might say, is being punished by getting what she wants. If she wants to forget, she will be escorted away "to the place she had always longed to be; she had slipped back in time to a point where her husband did not exist in either memory or desire and where consequently she felt neither pressure nor remorse" (*BLF* 175–76). In fact, an allusion to Kafka's Gregor Samsa is evident as Tamina departs with Raphael at the beginning of this section of the narration. When Tamina agrees (to Raphael's guidance) "in a dreamy voice" to go to this place "where things weigh nothing at all," the narrator steps in to tell us, "And as in a fairy-tale, as in a dream (no, it *is* a fairy-tale, it *is* a dream!), Tamina walks out from behind the corner" (164). Recalling the famous opening paragraph of Kafka's story, in which the narrator bluntly emphasizes, "It was no dream," the denial of simile or metaphor in these lines from Kundera's text ironically suggests the opposite of what they say, for fairy tales or dreams are, of course, highly metaphorical. These lines are also ironic because Tamina's departure with Raphael quickly changes from a meeting narrated in plausibly realistic fashion to a journey marked by signs of the mythic or the fantastic: she is guided across a body of water by a strange, sexually precocious boy and then resides on an island inhabited solely by children, where the narrative slips into an allegorical or fairy-tale-like unreality.

Tamina's ultimately fatal immersion in this world of literalized metaphor, or fairy tales come too frighteningly true, also serves to emphasize her inability to use metaphor or her imagination successfully to bridge the gap separating her from her past. Instead, she has repeatedly tried to re-create the past literally (by attempting to write a mirror copy of the lost notebooks and by planning to send people to retrieve the notebooks). Her failure suggests that such a literal return or recuperation is impossible and that, without an imaginative bridge, all access to the past is lost. Tamina fails to cross imaginatively over the geographic and temporal borders separating her from her past, and so she is led passively away into a metaphorical version of the kind of existence she has chosen for herself through this failure, an isolated island with no bridges of any kind, where she is condemned to a timeless, meaningless exile.[13]

The island represents a frightful parody of the Pioneer camps found "everywhere east of the Elbe" (*BLF* 173) and of utopian worlds built on innocence, inexperience, and the present tense. It is depicted as "enormously" different from the landscape she has left behind.[14] All is green here as if it were a giant playground. What Tamina notices is the diminutiveness of the entire place as symbolized by the volleyball nets that are too close to the ground. Children are the only occupants of this island, and thus all is catered to their needs. The dormitories contain big open rooms full of little beds. The lack of privacy is most notable at evening's washing. The children, divided by groups, labeled with animal names, partake in an organized bathroom ritual. Since Tamina stands out as the only mature person among these children, she soon becomes an object of sexual discovery. The children touch her body, exploring, probing, as if she were "an open watch or a fly whose wings had been torn off" (*BLF* 177). The wingless-fly simile foreshadows the switch that occurs in the minds of the children: the innocent touching suddenly leads to the desire to cause pain. The narrator explains this sudden shift: "Their only motive for causing pain to someone not of their world is to glorify that world and its law" (185). Of course, Tamina realizes that she can no longer function in this world of dwarfs playing hopscotch and provocatively dancing as if "imitating intercourse" (188) to the idiocy of guitars.[15] She decides to escape the children's island, a place that offers only the opposite of her previous existence, a buoyant meaningless present.

Tamina swims away.[16] But no shores appear and so she drowns. Despite Tamina's death, however, the ending provides some sense of optimism. After all, she does escape this meaningless world, unwilling to conform to the rules laid out by the children, unwilling to lose her memory fully and thus her identity.[17]

Yet another interpretive possibility comes to mind in regard to the children's island. The narrator's statement introducing the second part of Tamina's story, "as in a fairy-tale, as in a dream (no, it *is* a fairy-tale, it *is* a dream!)" (*BLF* 164), hints that all this indeed may be a dream. Given Tamina's situation, it would be atypical if she did not suffer from what may be termed émigré nightmares. These nightmares appear to most people who find themselves in exile, especially in the first few years. The basic situation presented in these dreams—all are quite similar and repetitive in nature—is that an émigré finds a way back to the home country. The realization that being here is dangerous comes very quickly to the émigré. A desperate journey back to the country of exile follows but generally fails. The émigré wakes up with a feeling of desperate homelessness and utter alienation.

The second part of Tamina's story follows the general pattern of such a dream. At first, Tamina finds a way to go back; the children's island represents the homeland, even if not fully recognizable. Of course, Tamina does not fit in; her situation even becomes dangerous when the children begin to hate her, and her need to leave this world grows stronger and stronger with each new day. Her attempt to swim back to the other shore, the country of exile, of freedom, fails. Tamina is left in between the two countries, helpless, alone, uncomprehended, and purposeless.

Kundera returns once more to the problem of preserving personal memory in exile in *The Unbearable Lightness of Being* (1984). Here, the heroine, Sabina, finds herself in an existential quandary analogous to Tamina's. She is an artist persistently in search of the "unintelligible truth" (*ULB* 63) and as such cannot live in an oppressive regime that dictates her every move, her every stroke of the brush. To gain artistic freedom, she leaves her homeland to join the ranks of exiles in the West. Unlike Tamina, who abandoned her diaries, Sabina takes along her most private possession, a bowler hat. This black bulky object, once a prop for her love games, unexpectedly acquires greater signifying power in exile; it turns into "a monument to time past" (87), evoking Sabina's personal past, her life in Czechoslovakia. As such, the bowler hat becomes a central image in this novel. This image embodies the problems of bridging and most profoundly reflects the tension between remembering and forgetting as experienced in exile.[18]

The bowler hat is a central image for the existential problem of memory, but it is an extremely ambiguous image too. Mirroring the interpretive complexity of the work as a whole, the hat appears in tandem with the perplexing philosophical questions posed at the outset of the novel, questions pertaining to Friedrich Nietzsche's idea of the eternal return and Parmenides' view of the world consisting of opposites.[19] The ambiguity is especially evident in one of the first descriptions of the hat's significance:

> It returned again and again, each time with a different meaning, and all the meanings flowed through the bowler hat like water through a riverbed. I might call it Heraclitus' ("You can't step twice into the same river") riverbed: the bowler hat was a bed through which each time Sabina saw another river flow, another *semantic river:* each time the same object would give rise to a new meaning, though all former meanings would resonate (like an echo, like a parade of echoes) together with the new one. Each new experience would resound, each time enriching the harmony. (*ULB* 88)

Here the narrator indirectly invokes the "mad myth" of the eternal return by emphasizing the object's persistent recurrence.[20] The bowler appears and reappears in Sabina's life and, by extension, in the text, but always in a different form because of its ever-shifting and ever-expanding meaning. The word *meaning,* reiterated in the above quotation, not only stylistically underlines the thematic repetition, it also points to a number of interpretive possibilities.[21] The array of interpretations can be categorized, according to Fred Miller Robinson, in terms of dualities (or Parmenidean opposites). In his study of the bowler hat's historical significance and artistic presentation, Robinson arrives at an innate contradiction contained within the hat's dark brim: a contradiction of the "comic individualist," as popularized by Charlie Chaplin, and of the "sedate conformist," as represented by the middle-class businessman.[22] Robinson then argues that this contradiction is reflected in Kundera's text as well. Here the hat's duality is expressed by its lightness because it is "the kind of hat Chaplin wore" (*ULB* 64), reminding Tomas and Sabina of their love games, and by its weight because it is "a monument to time past" (87), witnessing two centuries of historical upheaval. The hat is a "sign of gaiety and gravity, both a 'joke' (p. 86) and a memento."[23] As a memento, it inherently embodies the tension between remembering and forgetting. Yet these seemingly clear divisions—between lightness and weight, between joke and memento—frequently become blurred and even reversed.[24] The hat thus becomes a contradictory image, defying simple interpretation, but in its state of "weight," it becomes quite an appropriate image for the equally complex philosophical and existential issues of memory.[25]

The spectrum of tensions, contradictions, and even reversals of meaning manifests itself in the first textual presentation of the hat. The setting is exile, in a Zurich hotel, where the lovers Sabina and Tomas reunite following the Soviet occupation of their native land: "When she opened the door, she stood before him on her beautiful long legs wearing nothing but panties and bra. And a black bowler hat. She stood there staring, mute and motionless, Tomas did the same. Suddenly he realized how touched he was. He removed the bowler from her head and placed it on the bedside table. Then they made love without saying a word" (*ULB* 28). Sabina, the imaginative seductress, puts on the hat to accentuate her provocative attire. Intended to evoke a playfully erotic mood, the hat at first appears in its "light" form. However, the sensual abandonment so prevalent in all other love scenes (one only has to recall Sabina's visual fantasies or Tereza's piercing screams) never materializes during this rendezvous. Instead, the hat causes silence between the lovers, indicating an emotional state of being instead of an enraptured one. Moreover, the actual description of the love act is absent (an atypical phenomenon in Kundera's oeuvre), hinting at the narrator's own "silencing" of the erotic dimension. Although by now the reader suspects that the hat has been transformed into something more serious than a sexual prop, its significance remains unclear. Only some sixty pages later does the narrator return to this episode with an explanation: "The reason why Tomas and Sabina were touched by the sight of the bowler hat in a Zurich hotel and made love almost in tears was that its black presence was not merely a reminder of their love games but also a memento of Sabina's father and of her grandfather, who lived in a century without airplanes and cars" (88). In exile, the hat has gained in significance. It has come to represent a past that is woven from all its owners' lives and from the history of the nation, a past that is "weighty" with memory.

This past, dating to the nineteenth century (the same century the bowler was designed), begins with the figure of Sabina's grandfather, the first owner of the hat and the mayor of a small town in Bohemia: "Sabina had never known him; all he'd left behind was this bowler hat and a picture showing a raised platform with several small-town dignitaries on it; one of them was Grandfather; it wasn't at all clear what they were doing up there on the platform; maybe they were officiating at some ceremony, unveiling a monument to a fellow dignitary who had also once worn a bowler hat at public ceremonies" (65). As the old photograph documents, the bowler hat's original function was to convey dignity, honor, and respectability, in other words, a certain social status. With time, however, this function has disappeared. The twentieth century has brought about not only technological changes, such as cars and airplanes, but also a new name for the country, Czechoslovakia. And as indicated by the renaming, the country undergoes its share of events: domination by the Austro-Hungarian monarchy, then by Germany; involvement in both world wars; the Communist takeover; and finally, occupation by Soviet troops. The proprietorship of the hat falls to Sabina's father, who lives in the same small town but under a political regime that no longer tolerates mayors or bowler hats, both now regarded as bourgeois anachronisms. Thus, unlike the grandfather, the father occupies no important official post. Instead, he spends his whole life painting "woodland sunsets and roses in vases" (91). Sabina's father, strict and puritanical, finds no use for the black object, and so it remains purposeless and forgotten.

However, the life of the hat is also fashioned with a more recent fabric. Sabina, unwilling to quibble over her deceased parents' possessions, defiantly claims it as her sole inheritance. Under her ownership, the hat goes through a series of physical displacements. First, it leaves the small town to accompany Sabina to an art studio in Prague. Here, no longer signifying dignity and seriousness, it acquires the most buoyant of its meanings: it becomes a prop for her love games with Tomas. Later, in a decision necessitated by the political events of the 1968 Soviet invasion, the bowler is chosen from among more practical objects to relocate abroad. This privileging of an awkward and bulky object over something of monetary value, which would be so needed in exile, points not only to Sabina's consciously cultivated originality but also to her strong sense of personal and cultural heritage. The hat serves as a reminder of its owners and their aspirations, as well as of the nation's two centuries of cultural and political upheavals. Therefore, when Sabina finds herself alone with Tomas in a Zurich hotel room, far away from their homeland, the hat suddenly evokes memories of this past. In a sense, the heroine, by carrying the hat with her into exile, indicates her reluctance to part (at least initially) with her past.

Sabina's personally and historically "weighty" bowler proves an artistic asset while she is in exile. Cognizant of two cultures and their respective settings (ex-homeland, country of exile), she acquires what Said terms a "plurality of vision" (55). Her attraction to New York manifests this unique double vision:

> The view changed with each step, . . . a fountain spurting water and a group of construction workers sitting on the rim eating lunch; strange iron ladders running up and down buildings with ugly red facades, so ugly that they were beautiful; and next door, a huge glass skyscraper backed by another, itself topped by a small Arabian pleasure-dome with turrets, galleries, and gilded columns.
>
> She was reminded of her paintings. There, too, incongruous things came together: a steelworks construction site superimposed on a kerosene lamp; an old-fashioned lamp with a painted-glass shade shattered into tiny splinters and rising up over a desolate landscape of marshland. (*ULB* 101)

The juxtaposition of New York's architecture and Sabina's paintings results in the artist's ability to perceive even the most mundane things, things that are usually taken for granted by native inhabitants, in a new and defamiliarizing light. This double-exposed vision, merging the present and the past, the unfamiliar and the familiar, brings Sabina both artistic and financial success in the West. As we learn in the course of the novel, she "had no trouble selling her paintings" (273). In addition, on the personal level, Sabina's existential outlook affords her a sense of security, embodied by the bowler: no matter where she goes, Sabina carries her homeland along, provided her past can be retrieved through memories. Even New York becomes "the secret but authentic homeland of her painting" (102).

Just as Sabina's past can serve as a unique and enriching part of her life, so can it easily be misunderstood, especially by those who do not share a similar background. The artist's past becomes a point of misperception, as symbolized by the inability of another of her lovers, Franz, to decipher the hat's significance. Rich with personal and cultural history that predates Franz, in his presence the hat is transformed into "an incomprehensible gesture" (88), an object devoid of all meaning:

> Near the mirror stood a wig stand with an old black bowler hat on it. She bent over, picked up the hat, and put it on her head. The image in the mirror was instantaneously transformed: suddenly it was a woman in her undergarments, a beautiful, distant, indifferent woman with a terribly out-of-place bowler hat on her head, holding the hand of a man in a gray suit and a tie.
>
> Again he had to smile at how poorly he understood his mistress. When she took her clothes off, it wasn't so much erotic provocation as an odd little caper, a happening à deux. His smile beamed understanding and consent.
>
> He waited for his mistress to respond in kind, but she did not. Without letting go of his hand, she stood staring into the mirror, first at herself, then at him.
>
> The time for the happening had come and gone. Franz was beginning to feel that the caper (which, in and of itself, he was happy to think of as charming) had dragged on too long. So he gently took the brim of the bowler hat between two fingers, lifted it off Sabina's head with a smile, and laid it back on the wig stand. (85)

Here Sabina is trying to relive, through the bowler, her sexual past once shared with her former lover, Tomas. The bowler, however, is an empty vessel for Franz, and the "parade of echoes . . . enriching [the bowler's] harmony" (88) falls silent on his ears. Franz fails to respond to Sabina's beckoning.[26] Sabina, instead of painstakingly explaining the bowler's meaning, remains silent. Perhaps she is afraid that her explanations would be reductive or perhaps ineffective; either way, she leaves the cultural gap unbridged.[27] This idea that one's past and memories are incommunicable is further emphasized by the title of the part in which this episode appears, "Words Misunderstood." Finally, Franz's silent removal of the bowler hat from Sabina's head does not suffice to erase the semantic abyss, the communication gap, created between the two lovers. Soon after this episode, the Czech artist, whose life consists of "a long road of betrayals" (*ULB* 98), abandons the Swiss intellectual, and he remains clueless about her motives. Although Franz acquires a new young lover, emotionally he remains bound to Sabina, naively imagining her gaze to be set on him forever—naively, because Sabina's gaze becomes less and less directed at the past.

Sabina's fading interest in the past is appropriately accompanied by the bowler's disappearance from the text. Positioning herself more and more within the present time frame, she no longer values the hat, which was once meant to evoke memories of the past. In other words, it becomes an ordinary object, no longer worth mentioning. Such conscious and willful forgetting leads Sabina to the end of her "road of betrayals." She has now abandoned her homeland both physically and spiritually. Sabina is no longer able to understand or care about her fellow émigrés' retrospective glances and their preoccupation with a single historical moment: the 1968 Soviet invasion of Czechoslovakia. Unwilling to feel sorry for the "abandoned creatures they were" (98), abandoned because they failed to partake of the life of their new country, Sabina severs all ties with these émigrés. Such self-imposed alienation results in a disregard for her former homeland and its people. Unmoved by curiosity or concern, Sabina eventually stops reading the long letters from a small village in Czechoslovakia, from Simon (Tomas's son, with whom she corresponds). Finally, after becoming a "victim" of misrepresentation—of "a biography that read like the life of a saint or martyr: she had suffered, struggled against injustice, been forced to abandon her bleeding homeland, yet was carrying on the struggle" (254)—she hides her Czech nationality. In essence, Sabina is willing to go as far as erasing her past to avoid becoming the subject of kitsch.

Such manipulation and eventual obliteration of the past consequently result in a reductive existence for Sabina. Bergson's description of the adverse effects caused by grounding oneself only in the present aptly explains the risks Sabina faces: "Now let us relax the strain, let us interrupt the effort to crowd as much as possible of the past into the present. If the relaxation were complete, there would no longer be either memory or will—which amounts to saying that, in fact, we never do fall into this absolute passivity, any more than we can make ourselves absolutely free. But, in the limit, we get a glimpse of an existence made of a present which recommences unceasingly—devoid of real duration, nothing but the instantaneous which dies and is born again endlessly."[28] Here again, the heroine of *The Book of Laughter and Forgetting* comes to mind. The children's island on which Tamina spends her last days is just such a world, a world devoid of real duration. Tamina, like the children, is governed only by the repetitive present moment. No longer obsessed with her memories, she falls into the other extreme: she becomes devoid of a past. Such existence, ruled by the unbearable absence of weight, proves to be meaningless. Similarly, Sabina joins the children's world, becoming the adopted daughter of a doting elderly American couple. The old man observes "every stroke of her brush," and the old woman calls Sabina "my daughter" (*ULB* 255). The artist's metamorphosis into a "child" represents an escape from responsibilities, albeit a temporary one: the old man will soon die, and his wife will abandon Sabina for her own son. And again, as in *The Book of Laughter and Forgetting,* such existence is ephemeral. Although the artist's death is not presented overtly, her fear of it is: "She was afraid of shutting herself into a grave and sinking into American earth" (*ULB* 273).

Sabina's vague and metaphorical end stands in sharp contrast to some of the other characters' (even the dog's) deaths, which are rendered in minute detail. In other words, the narrative thread describing Sabina's life seems to be abandoned and forgotten by the narrator, as if reflecting the heroine's own willful forgetting. And while her disappearance from the text corresponds to that of the hat, the hat's last emergence (preceding Sabina's fear "of shutting herself into a grave" by some twenty pages) offers one of the most provocatively interpretive moments in the novel: "In Part Three of this novel I told the tale of Sabina standing half-naked with a bowler hat on her head and the fully dressed Tomas at her side. There is something I failed to mention at the time. While she was looking at herself in the mirror, excited by her self-denigration, she had a fantasy of Tomas seating her on the toilet in her bowler hat and watching her void her bowels. Suddenly her heart began to pound and, on the verge of fainting, she pulled Tomas down to the rug and immediately let out an orgasmic shout" (247). This passage, on the one hand, brings us back to the other, "lighter" meaning of the bowler, its erotic quality based on excitement. On the other hand, the initial lines are a narratological recall strategically leading the reader not only to part 3 but also back to the beginning of the novel. And now the bowler's connection to the Nietzschean eternal return comes into sharper focus: "Putting it negatively, the myth of eternal return states that a life which disappears once and for all, which does not return, is like a shadow, without weight, dead in advance, and whether it was horrible, beautiful, or sublime, its horror, sublimity, and beauty mean nothing" (3). As Nina Pelikan Straus claims, Kundera articulates a longing for Nietzsche's repetitive version of history because, despite its monotony, it still allows for resistance against a life "which disappears once and for all, which does not return," and in the end means nothing (*ULB* 3).[29] A history characterized by eternal return confronts and resists the temptation of the unbearable lightness of living without memory and thus without meaning. As long as Sabina cherishes her past and her memories as those that grant her the unique double vision of an exile, her life is rich with meaning and significance. But once her past is forgotten and left behind, Sabina's presence, along with her bowler hat, fades out of the text.

The protagonist's fading out of the text, whether due to voluntary forgetting, as is the case with Sabina, or involuntary memory lapses, as is the case with Tamina, serves as a frightening reminder that one must incessantly struggle to preserve the past in order to meet a fate different from Sabina's or Tamina's. Although Kundera has not presented us with a fictional émigré who successfully balances the past with the present, I believe that the narrative itself suggests a way to achieve this bridge.[30] The structural layout of *The Unbearable Lightness of Being* implies a way of reading that successfully weaves the past into the present.[31]

In the opening lines of *The Unbearable Lightness of Being*, Kundera's introduction to Nietzsche's idea of the eternal return—the philosophical discussion based on the concept of repetition—provides more than a philosophical grounding. It pervades and informs the text not only through the repetition of images, as we have seen, for example, in the analysis of the bowler hat, but also through the innovative play of narrative frequency on the structural level of the text. In fact, repetition dominates the form of this novel. Based on a seven-part structure, *The Unbearable Lightness of Being* displays its repetitive pattern even in the table of contents.[32] Two of the part titles are duplicated, "Lightness and Weight" (parts 1 and 5) and "Soul and Body" (parts 2 and 4).[33] Moreover, within these four parts, the events of the plot are narrated twice, each time from a different perspective and with a different style. For example, in the "Lightness and Weight" parts, dedicated to Tomas, the narrative unfolds through philosophical, linguistic, musical, mythological, and historical passages or short essays; whereas, in the "Soul and Body" parts, which center on Tereza, dream sequences and anatomical reflections are woven into the narrative.

However, narrative frequency is also evident in the way that events, scenes, and sentences are sometimes repeated verbatim or with only slight variations, as well as in the broader structural organization of the novel.[34] An interesting example of a small-scale repetition is that of the image of the bulrush basket, which shows both the complexity of this narrative technique and a way of reading this text. The basket emerges early on, in Tomas's first impressions of Tereza: "He had come to feel an inexplicable love for this all but complete stranger; she seemed a child to him, a child someone had put in a bulrush basket daubed with pitch and sent downstream for Tomas to fetch at the riverbank of his bed" (*ULB* 6).

A few pages later, the narrator repeats this thought with only slight stylistic and linguistic variations (this time, a segment of the passage is in the conditional tense rather than in the past): "Again it occurred to him that Tereza was a child put in a pitch-daubed bulrush basket and sent downstream. He couldn't very well let a basket with a child in it float down a stormy river! If the Pharaoh's daughter hadn't snatched the basket carrying little Moses from the waves . . ." (10–11). Here the myth of an abandoned child floating down the river is elaborated, and the narrator lets us know that Tomas is thinking of Tereza specifically in biblical terms.

In the opening to part 5, the myth is mentioned again, now expanding its boundaries to include the story of Oedipus:

When Tereza unexpectedly came to visit Tomas in Prague, he made love to her, as I pointed out in Part One, that very day, or rather, that very hour, but suddenly thereafter she became feverish. As she lay in his bed and he stood over her, he had the irrepressible feeling that she was a child who had been put in a bulrush basket and sent downstream to him.

The image of the abandoned child had consequently become dear to him, and he often reflected on the ancient myths in which it occurred. It was apparently with this in mind that he picked up a translation of Sophocles' *Oedipus*. (175)

As is evident from the above quotations, each consecutive recurrence adds more possible meanings to the initial comparison of Tereza to a child found in a basket, so that this image grows semantically richer and more complex each time it appears. Additionally, these quotations reveal a deliberate attempt to make the reader aware of the earlier descriptions, which increases the complexity of the repetitiveness even more.[35] Allusions to previous mentions are emphasized through the use of such phrases as "again it occurred to him" and the even more explicit "as I pointed out in Part One." In other words, the narrative openly retraces its own path, a device Gérard Genette calls the repeating analepses or recalls.[36]

This gesturing back is used so prominently in the novel that one is encouraged not only to acknowledge the frequent replaying of events but actually to return in his or her reading and compare the various versions of the same event. In an early passage, the narrator describes Sabina's shifting interpretations of the bowler hat as readings of "semantic rivers," explaining that various meanings flow "through the bowler hat like water through a riverbed" (*ULB* 88). So too the reader must navigate his or her way through the river of the narrative as it increasingly broadens its banks, swelling with meaning through the addition of each consecutive repetition. The reader is thus unable to proceed in an easy linear fashion through the fragmented and achronological text.

The structural principle of repetition (and recall) challenges the reader's process of remembering.[37] As reader-response critics have demonstrated, the process of reading is one in which all readers constantly bridge gaps and make connections, at least on a subconscious level, to themes or images encountered earlier.[38] Kundera's narrative strategy both enacts and foregrounds this process so that the reader is led to a greater conscious awareness of the repetition and thus to an awareness of the importance of carrying the past forward as one reads. The present and future time of reading thereby becomes richer, denser, and more meaningful.

This narratological play with frequency underscores the thematic attention to personal memory as well. In other words, the thematic repetition of the image of the bowler hat is, as I have argued, linked to the possibility that Sabina will do (although she fails to do) what Kundera encourages his readers to do: to carry or remember the past as one moves forward into the future. Just as the bowler hat keeps reappearing in Sabina's life, each time embodying a different meaning, so does the text's structure keep challenging the reader to piece the past narrative fragments together to determine meaning. *The Unbearable Lightness of Being* asks the reader to be involved. Recalls are the bowler hat for the reader; without the recalls, the reader gets a kitschy, linear reading, a less rich, less dense text, just as without the bowler hat Sabina is reduced to a disconnected existence as the adopted child, of sorts, of an elderly American couple, stripped and separated from any authentic and meaningful relationship to her past.

Kundera's two heroines' inability to imaginatively link their personal memories with their present lives looms darkly over them. Letters, diaries, photographs, and bowler hats keep reappearing throughout the characters' lives, yet these personal mementos do not signal a creative or cognitive moment. They function only as cherished fragments from the past, fragments that remain unconnected to the present. Since imagination is not called on for appropriating these mementos into the heroine's present lives, they are less and less often mentioned in the text. Eventually they turn into meaningless objects, corresponding to the emptiness experienced by their owners. Personal mementos come to symbolize forgetting a theme that is as weighty as remembering.

Part Two: *Cultural Memory*

Culture dies only for those who fail to master it, the way morality dies for a lecher.

—Joseph Brodsky, "Why Milan Kundera
Is Wrong about Dostoyevsky"

3. Vladimir Nabokov:
Writers Blind and Dangerous

Brodsky's premise, that culture is indeed a possession, is in fact the only possession worth having, holds true especially for the first wave of Russian emigration.[1] Determined not to have Russian literature confiscated by the new Soviet government, many intellectuals emigrated not only to pursue their own individual freedom of expression but to preserve and expand their cultural heritage abroad. Russian publishing houses sprang up around major European cities, Prague, Berlin, Paris, allowing scientific, religious, poetic, and philosophical writings to flourish. The importance of writing and publishing as a means of personal intellectual outlet and as a means of cultural augmentation beyond the Russian borders became a topos for Nabokov.[2] In the novels discussed here, *Mary* and *The Gift*, two fictional writers approach their cultural heritage in opposing manners. One man cannot sustain his rich heritage due to an overwhelming passivity that plagues his present existence, while the other fosters imaginative links to his cultural past in order to transform the bleak presence of exile into a fertile territory. It is through the fates of these two characters that Nabokov convinces us of Brodsky's premise that culture does indeed overcome life's hardships and that without culture one is groundless and possessionless.

Nabokov dedicates his first novel, *Mary*, to the treacherous terrain of groundlessness, characterized by cultural vastness. As I mentioned in chapter 1, Ganin is the only character who successfully escapes the unstable pension in Berlin, which is a transit station between Russia and the new, desired destination in exile. Yet the pension is full of other Russian émigrés who cannot leave this temporary transit station. These dwellers are static because they spend their time dreaming of someone or someplace else.[3] Podtyagin, the old poet who most explicitly embodies their fate, is unable to write poetry, work for a publishing house, or move beyond the shaking walls of the pension because he both neglects to pay attention to his new environment and fails to foster connections to his past, ties to a cultural memory that would grant him the strength and reason necessary to move into the future. His futile hopes are evident in his frequent exclamation: "I only hope to God I can get to Paris. Life is more free and easy there" (*M* 54). As Connolly points out, Podtyagin's dream of a happier future in another place is reminiscent of the repeated cry of Irina and her sisters in Anton Chekhov's *Three Sisters:* "Let us go to Moscow! I implore you, let us go. There is nothing in the world better than Moscow!" (*N'sEF* 33). The allusion to Chekhov suggests that Podtyagin's Paris operates as a kind of substitute for a lost Russia (the sisters' Moscow), as if this émigré's idealized Paris in some way stands in place of the now only imagined homeland.[4] For the old poet, then, Paris and Moscow cease to represent tangible geographic locations; instead, these signifiers of unattainable cities ironically serve only to emphasize how he is dislocated, floundering in an abyss between two unreal territories that leaves him with no stable grounding in the present.[5]

However, Podtyagin's unfulfilled dream of a future place and life is far more complex and poignant than the musings of Chekhov's three sisters. He is also beset by sudden, unpremeditated dreams and recollections of his abandoned homeland, which, although physically lost to the Bolsheviks, maintains an unrelenting hold on him. For example, as noted in chapter 1, while enjoying a cup of tea in the Berlin pension, he spoons up a lump of sugar and muses that "there was something Russian about that little porous lump, something rather like the melting snow in springtime" (*M* 54). This tie to the past is not based merely on personal recollections or flashbacks, as was the case with Ganin, whose most profound experience in his homeland was a deeply personal love affair. Podtyagin's links to Russia are indicative of a broader cultural experience. In the past, he was a poet of lyrical verses about birch trees. Given that birch trees are a heartfelt symbol of the Russian countryside, the image suggests that Podtyagin's poetry had deep roots in his native soil. The tenacity of these roots is reflected in his desperate clinging to anything that is associated with his homeland. He lives with fellow émigrés, cultivates only Russian friendships, and wants to settle in Paris not because it is the chosen destination of his exile but because his Russian niece lives there.

Yet these links to his past do not come together in any creative, sustained, productive, nourishing way. At times, Podtyagin idealizes his past; more often, however, his reveries haunt him "as something monstrous" (81). Both types of reverie produce no tangible result. In fact, direct contacts with his past only leave him passively upset, confused, and unable to write. When his old school friend Kunitsyn visits, Podtyagin feels insulted by his offer of money, sad about the childhood memories evoked, and, in general, out of sorts: "It was impossible to tell what he was thinking about: whether it was about the dullness of his past life; or whether old age, illness and poverty had risen before his mind's eyes with the same dark clarity as the reflection in the nighttime window" (43). I argue in the introduction that a successful émigré artistic vision is one that creates a kaleidoscope, combining the fragments of past memories with the light made possible by a clear outlook on the present. But here the opposite is the case. Images of past and present remain only dull and meaningless (impossible to "read") in Podtyagin's mind. With only an oxymoronic "dark clarity" for illumination, his émigré existence remains plagued by shadows.

To further complicate things, Podtyagin, haunted by painful fragments of a past that emerge in disturbing, confusing ways, also consciously and willfully severs one of the most potentially important and productive connections to his past cultural identity. In a revealing moment of what the narrator calls good-natured irony, the old poet summarizes his past professional life and winds up completely cutting any links to a cultural past that once provided his life with meaning. He explains, "What a fool I was— for the sake of those birch trees I wasted all my life, I overlooked the whole of Russia. Now, thank God, I've stopped writing poetry. Done with it" (41). However, in the course of the novel, we learn that Podtyagin's life was not wasted, for his poems were widely published, quoted in love letters, and even remembered by others in exile, like Ganin: "It occurred to him that Podtyagin nevertheless had bequeathed something, even if nothing more than the two pallid verses which had blossomed into such warm, undying life for him, Ganin, in the same way as a cheap perfume or the street signs in a familiar street become dear to us" (110). Ganin's memory of Podtyagin's verses suggests the poet's power, the power to evoke and preserve a memory of a native land that can no longer be visited. Thus, even Ganin, the ultimate loner, is connected through Podtyagin's poetry to a place and a nation, and from this link he is able to draw strength, "warm, undying life." For Podtyagin to downplay his role and cultural importance by jettisoning any possibly useful links to this past means that he is not willing to foster an imaginative or poetic response to his present situation. And in fact, his present is characterized by cultural absence. He admits to abandoning an émigré publishing venture in Berlin and relinquishing his poetic pen. He not only cuts himself off from a cultural environment that is inherently provided by a publishing house and by remaining in the poets' ranks but, more important, he willingly silences his own voice and the voices of others (by not providing a means of appearing in print).[6] This failure is especially acute because, as an artist, Podtyagin is uniquely positioned to explore creatively the pitfalls and potentials of the émigré condition.

The effects of his loss of control over the personal and cultural memories that would sustain him in exile—and the dangerous consequences of this loss—are strikingly evident in Podtyagin's corporeal body. In contrast to Ganin's recuperation of a vital, energized physical self once he successfully negotiates the terrain between past and present, Podtyagin becomes increasingly disabled throughout the novel. The old poet, described as a "huge, soft doll" with a face "the color of clay" (*M* 61), keeps collapsing into weak fits of wheezing, fits that occur after episodes linked to the sudden reemergence of the past. In fact, he has a heart attack following an old schoolmate's visit and another one soon after a nightmare about St. Petersburg, as if painfully overcome by the fragments of his past.

Podtyagin's deteriorating, physical weakness is also evident in his myopia, a condition for which he dons not spectacles but pince-nez. Whenever he appears in the novel, the narrator notes his eyes glaring from behind the lenses of his pince-nez, or eyes "bare and blind without their pince-nez" (61). The choice of pince-nez rather than spectacles as corrective eyewear is noteworthy, for it signifies more than a physical defect. At the time in which the action of *Mary* takes place, 1924, pince-nez (developed in the 1840s) were no longer a popular choice for corrective lenses (their popularity was at its highest in the latter part of the nineteenth century). Sporting pince-nez, the old poet looks anachronistic, like a nineteenth-century Russian aristocrat displaced into the twentieth century, his eyewear operating as a symbol of the ways in which Podtyagin does not fit into the time and cultural setting in which he must make his way, signaling that he is not attuned to his present environment.

Pince-nez, representing a limited or monocular perspective, also suggest Podtyagin's misguided understanding of his present environment. He is "blinded" by his wistful dreams of some other time or of someplace else, dreams that cause his focus on the present to blur. It is this mental predicament of "blindness," his failure to direct his gaze at the current realities of his life as an émigré in Berlin and thus to understand his new cultural setting, that most directly destroys the old poet's chance of escaping to any kind of different future.

Podtyagin's disregard for his present environment is exemplified by his dealings with the German bureaucracy as he seeks to secure a visa for further passage West. The country's machinery, with its endless files, forms, queues, and stamps, seems incomprehensible, Kafkaesque at first. Podtyagin is chased from one place to another, endlessly circling between officials, unable to explain what he wants, progressing nowhere. Yet at a closer glance, it turns out that the old poet's failure is due neither to the monstrous bureaucracy nor to his broken German but to his own unwillingness to get to know this country and its culture. A conversation with one of the fellow boarders, Alfyorov, best displays this lack of interest:

> "Today I had already begun to hope: ah, they will stamp my passport with their exit visa! Nothing of the sort. They sent me to have my picture taken, but the photos won't be ready until this evening."
>
> "All very proper," Alfyorov nodded. "That's how things should be in a well-run country. . . . Generally speaking, the difference between our country and this one can be expressed like this: imagine a curve, and on it—" . . .
>
> "I don't quite understand your geometry," Podtyagin was saying, carefully sweeping bread crumbs into the palm of his hand with his knife. . . .
>
> "But don't you see? It's so clear," cried Alfyorov excitedly. "Just imagine—"
>
> "I don't understand it," Podtyagin repeated firmly, and, tilting his head back slightly, he poured the collection of crumbs into his mouth. (15)

Podtyagin's stubborn interruptions of Alfyorov's genuine attempts to explain the logic of Germany prevent Podtyagin from gaining any insight into his present condition. It is as if he desires to remain uninformed, in the dark. Moreover, Alfyorov's question—"Don't you see?"—suggests that indeed Podtyagin does not want to see his present surroundings.

Alfyorov's futile attempt to enlighten the old poet about German bureaucracy is followed by Ganin's guidance of the old poet through the maze of offices. It is noteworthy that in classical literature it is the old man who guides the younger one. Here the condition of exile reverses this situation. It is the old poet who is more helpless than the younger man in a new environment, unable to adapt to change or even to notice it. In the following scene, it becomes apparent that the old man has paid no attention to simple instructions, that he has indeed been blind to his surroundings: "'You must stand in the queue and get a number,' said Ganin. 'And I never did that before,' the old poet replied in a whisper. 'I just used to go straight in through the door'" (79). With Ganin in charge, the German officials are defeated. Podtyagin, trustfully shuffling behind his guide, does obtain the long-awaited passport. Moreover, the whole affair is accomplished quickly and effortlessly.

The last part of Podtyagin's journey—to secure his visa for what seems an imminent departure—is one last stamp from the French consulate. Podtyagin, while examining the photograph in his passport during a bus ride, suddenly looks away, directing his glance at a different time and space. He retells the dream he had of St. Petersburg the night before.

> I was walking along the Nevski. I knew it was the Nevski, although it looked nothing like it. The houses had sloping angles as in a futurist painting, and the sky was black, although I knew it was daytime. And the passers-by were giving me strange looks. Then a man crossed the street and took aim at my head. He's an old haunter of mine. It's terrible—oh, terrible—that whenever we dream about Russia we never dream of it as beautiful, as we know it was in reality, but as something monstrous—the sort of dreams where the sky is falling in and you feel the world's coming to an end. (81)

This dream, an émigré nightmare, depicts the old poet's place back in the homeland as terrifying, even deadly. Yet it not only evokes the danger of physically returning to Russia but also foreshadows the potential danger of dreams interfering with, even destroying, one's present existence.[7] Indeed, Podtyagin stops paying attention to his immediate circumstance and fails to be observant about his passport. It is precisely at this moment that he loses the document. Thus the dream, even if only indirectly, leads to the loss of both the passport and the possibility of ever escaping the transit station, the pension in Berlin. The old poet later explains his mistake with a pathetic allusion to the Russian futurist poets, sadly referring to his lost "license" in terms of poetic "license": "That's it: I dropped it. Poetic license: elided passport. 'The trousered Cloud' by [Vladimir] Mayakovsky. Great big clouded cretin, that's what I am" (*M* 84). It is ironic that Podtyagin uses a reference to a futurist poet to mock his own clumsiness, because the futurists would have had nothing to do with an outdated poet like him, and now he will have no future—at least not one in Paris as he had dreamed. Eric Laursen emphasizes this link between a lack of license and a lack of future freedom in the West, pointing out that, in the original Russian, poetic license *(poeticheskaia vol'nost)* also means poetic freedom.[8]

The loss of the passport is followed soon after by the old poet's death. His last words to Ganin express his tragic dislocatedness: "'You see—without any passport.' Something like faint mirth twisted his lips. He screwed up his eyes again and once more the abyss sucked him down" (*M* 109). He falls into the abyss of the present, between Russia and France. Podtyagin thus represents the fate of a person who cannot find a stable footing in exile. He is unable to carry his homeland with him in the form of either personal or cultural memories, unable to utilize his poetic freedom, which would grant the present environment of Berlin meaning. Fragments of his past keep invading, interfering with the present, yet these memories are not revitalizing but only lead to despair and loss. Without a rich and useful link to a past, an émigré like Podtyagin has no resource upon which to rely as he moves into the future. In addition, he mistakenly disregards his present existence, forgetting that Berlin is a necessary bridge suspended between two shores, between past and future. To cross this bridge and to make Paris more than a dream, more than Moscow was for Chekhov's three sisters, Podtyagin needs to enrich his present—the only "bridge" available to him—by a possession that gave him purpose and aspiration.

The difficulty of spanning the treacherous terrain of exile, the challenge of carrying the past into the present so as to enable a successful future, is also at play in *The Gift*, written more than ten years after *Mary*. In this later novel, however, the old fictional poet Podtyagin is replaced by Fyodor, a young émigré writer who is searching actively for a poetic voice that would sustain his talent in exile. Fyodor's ambition to become a successful writer, not silenced by his new cultural surroundings, takes him on several journeys down the path of memory. He explores the artistic potential of literary works based on personal memories in both his early poetry collection and his attempted biography of his father, Konstantin. And even though these early endeavors too are influenced by a "working through" of Russian literary history, it is when Fyodor overtly turns to such a history—by writing a biography of Nikolay Chernyshevsky—that he best understands how he needs the imaginative sustenance afforded by strong ties with his cultural past to achieve his literary ambitions. Fyodor journeys into this cultural heritage to combine the resources of past writers and thinkers with his own still-limited experience. He is thus able to tap into a wider tradition, enriching his own poetic voice to develop a creative constellation of past, present, and future.

Fyodor's journey into cultural history has an unlikely destination: the distant past of committed litterateurs. The choice of subject matter for Fyodor's new biography puzzles many of his émigré friends. One of them even suggests a different literary figure for his work: "Why, you ought to write—I don't know— say, the life of [Konstantin] Batyushkov or [Anton] Delvig, something in the orbit of Pushkin—but what's the point of Chernyshevski?" (*G* 200).[9] But what his friend suggests, to focus on Pushkin's world (the first few decades of the early 1900s), is something that Fyodor has already explored. The biography of his father, described in chapter 2 of *The Gift*, is both inspired by Pushkin's "transparent rhythm of Arzrum" (*G* 108) and stylistically modeled after the great writer.[10] Of course, his friend knows nothing about this previous literary undertaking, since it remains in "drafts and extracts rammed under the linen in [Fyodor's] suitcase" (*G* 157). There the papers rest because of Fyodor's dissatisfaction with the limits he faced while writing this previous biography, for he admits to losing a sense of artistic distance, "that critical measure of detachment which the writer requires when giving completion to the inner life of another" (*N'sEF* 202).

Yet Fyodor's dissatisfaction with his former literary attempt is not the only reason he wants to extend his interests beyond Pushkin. The decision is also motivated by a desire to gain a more comprehensive understanding of his cultural background. This desire calls for a journey into the more distant and foreign territory of nineteenth-century Russian literature, a territory about which he has only questions:

> Suddenly he felt a bitter pang—why had everything in
> Russia become so shoddy, so crabbed and gray, how
> could she have been so befooled and befuddled? Or had
> the old urge "toward the light" concealed a fatal flaw,
> which in the course of progress toward the objective had
> grown more and more evident, until it was revealed that
> this "light" was burning in the window of a prison over-
> seer, and that was all? When had this strange dependence
> sprung up between the sharpening of thirst and the mud-
> dying of the source? In the forties? in the sixties? and
> "what to do" now? Ought one not to reflect any longing
> for one's homeland, for any homeland besides that which
> is with me, within me, which is stuck like the silver sand
> of the sea to the skin of my soles, lives in my eyes, my
> blood, gives depth and distance to the background of
> life's every hope? (*G* 187)

Fyodor's decision to try to answer these questions by writing a biography of Chernyshevsky is an artistic choice—and a political one—that seems surprising indeed. Surprising because Chernyshevsky (as presented by the author) is artistically "responsible for Russia's cultural wasteland" and politically responsible for contributing to a system that has indirectly necessitated Fyodor's own exile.[11] In fact, at the time in which the action of the novel takes place (the 1930s), the effects of the system of thought promulgated by this radical critic were at their most pernicious in the Soviet Union; many of Chernyshevsky's ideas about utilitarianism were put to use to articulate the harsh aesthetic doctrine of socialist realism. As Sergei Davydov notes, "Scores of independent and original talents were being physically annihilated in the Soviet Union" at the time of the writing of *The Gift*.[12] However, the move toward such an unexpected topic (the radicals of the 1960s, namely Chernyshevsky) is ironically influenced by Fyodor's previous work, the biography of his father, because Fyodor recalls and heeds his father's advice based on lepidopteral discoveries—that keen observation is of vital importance and that even a seemingly mundane subject can yield unexpected results.

Fyodor stumbles on the seemingly mundane topic of Chernyshevsky in a bookstore while reading literary reviews in émigré magazines about his favorite poet, Koncheyev. On another table, where Soviet editions are placed, Fyodor notices and picks up a chess magazine *(8 x 8)* because, as a chess composer, he feels compelled to solve chess problems. He spots an article entitled "Chernyshevski and Chess" and thinks it will amuse his fellow émigré Alexander Chernyshevsky (a namesake of the civic critic). However, it all turns out quite differently. The chess problems are uninteresting and offer no challenge, whereas the face of "a thin-bearded old man, glowering over his spectacles" intrigues Fyodor so much that he does not give the article to his friend. Instead, he himself starts reading the excerpted pieces of the civic critic's diary:

> He ran his eyes over the two-column extract from Chernyshevski's youthful diary; he glanced through it, smiled, and began to read it over with interest. The drolly circumstantial style, the meticulously inserted adverbs, the passion for semicolons, the bogging down of thought in mid sentence and the clumsy attempts to extricate it (whereupon it got stuck at once elsewhere, and the author had to start worrying it out all over again), the drubbing-in, rubbing-in tone of each word, the knight-moves of sense in the trivial commentary on his minutest actions, the viscid ineptitude of these actions (as if some workshop glue had got onto the man's hands, and both were left), the seriousness, the limpness, the honesty, the poverty— all this pleased Fyodor so much, he was so amazed and tickled by the fact that an author with such a mental and verbal style was considered to have influenced the literary destiny of Russia, that on the very next morning he signed out the complete works of Chernyshevski from the state library. (*G* 194–95)

The one long, sinuous sentence that describes how Fyodor happens upon his new topic of study is, to use Boyd's stylistic analogy, like a snake twisting and turning in a long-winded pattern (*VN:RY* 452). The snake image is apt here, for it recalls the father's discovery (Fyodor participates in this find through his imagination) of an undescribed species of a snake who "fed on mice, and the mouse I extracted from its stomach also turned out to be an undescribed species" (*G* 135). Keeping in mind that the father is an entomologist and that reptiles are not the main object of study during his long, difficult travels, it seems unexpected that he would notice the snake and then so carefully examine it. Yet Fyodor too stumbles on his find, Chernyshevsky's chess problems, by accident or fate. The civic critic, likewise, seems a strange subject to "dissect." Yet Fyodor follows both the father's example and his own artistic hunch, smiling as the father once did when embarking on something new, experiencing "a peculiar kind of bliss" (*G* 195) as he mulls over the writing task ahead.

This "bliss" is not merely associated with the revelation of a new (for Fyodor) "species" of literary figure. In Fyodor's case, it will also lead to self-discovery, to a sharper awareness of the pitfalls and potentials of his own condition in exile. What Fyodor unexpectedly realizes in the midst of his new writing project is that Chernyshevsky repeatedly fails to take advantage of journeys by neglecting to remain attentive to and appreciative of the changing environments that he experiences while traveling across the seas to England or into Siberian exile. Fyodor explores how this inattentiveness only exacerbates Chernyshevsky's failure and decline in exile, leaving him a broken man, trapped and ineffectual. Now Fyodor's challenge, one that faces all émigrés, is to understand how best to make a journey a successful experience, how best to move beyond the boundaries of known territories to face the challenges of the unknown. Fyodor emphasizes that how one travels says much about how one survives or succeeds in exile, stressing important lessons about how one can make the most out of this condition through keen observation, a trait Chernyshevsky never exhibits or fosters.

In fact, Fyodor's acute awareness of how he risks sharing the same fate Chernyshevsky suffered, that of a failed, stagnant existence in exile, may help explain the dramatic change in tone from Fyodor's description of his protagonist's life early in the biography to the account of his forced exile in Siberia. The biography begins in a tone that is parodic, ironic, and at times even cruel. But as Connolly has observed, Fyodor's tone "softens somewhat after Chernyshevski is sent into exile" (207). Connolly suggests that this may be because Chernyshevsky's painful distance from his family reminds Fyodor of his own father's frequent absences and final disappearance or that the relationship between the civic critic and his son Sasha "provides a tragic shadow for the Konstantin–Fyodor relationship" (207). However, another reason behind the softening of tone in this part of the biography may be that Fyodor's own experience of exile leads him to consider Chernyshevsky's fate with tenderer empathy.[13]

Nonetheless, this empathy does not prevent Fyodor from repeatedly emphasizing that Chernyshevsky's inattentiveness is partly to blame for his troubles. For example, in his depiction of the civic critic's journey to Siberia in a tarantass (a carriage), Fyodor writes that Chernyshevsky feels frustrated not because he is sent off to exile but because, "'to read books on the way' was permitted only beyond Irkutsk" (*G* 296).[14] Consequently, for the first one and one-half months of the journey, the unfortunate Chernyshevsky is bored, for he cannot conceive of another travel activity other than reading. This obsession with books—Fyodor refers to his protagonist as "a glutton for books" (225)—is already at play in Chernyshevsky's first trip from his hometown, Saratov, to St. Petersburg. Even in this earlier journey, Fyodor stresses that the young man pays no attention to the environment beyond his carriage window but instead only quietly reads a book, looking for the meaning of life in its pages rather than directing an inquisitive gaze to the wider world around him. Fyodor, narrating this scenario, cannot refrain from an ironic comment: "The landscape hymned by Gogol' passed unnoticed before the eyes of the eighteen-year-old Nikolay Gavrilovich. . . . It goes without saying that he preferred his 'war of words' to the 'corn ears bowing in the dust'" (226). The choice of vocabulary in this passage—"war of words"—indicates that, for Chernyshevsky, reading a book is a more real experience than observing his surroundings. The mention of Gogol not only reminds the reader of Fyodor's appropriation of Gogolian style in this biography but also suggests a connection to *Dead Souls* and Chichikov, who also traveled across the country yet who noticed everything, even if it was for his financial profit.[15]

His arrival in Siberia brings about neither the end of Chernyshevsky's travels nor any improvement in his habits of observation. Certainly, his situation is described as a difficult one. He is subjected to frequent resettlement within the region, and he no longer has a permanent place to call home, becoming a prisoner who has no control over his movements or destination. This situation is underscored by Fyodor's style. At this point in the biography, Fyodor chooses passive verb constructions, such as "He had been removed to Siberia" (*G* 293); "Chernyshevski was transferred to Aleksandrovski Zavod" (297); "He was taken to Krasnoyarsk, from there to Orenburg" (305). Since throughout the rest of the biography Fyodor uses active verb constructions, here the passivity on the stylistic level underlines and mirrors the thematic level, Chernyshevsky's own inertia, inertia that prevents him from making anything out of his condition.

Because of his passivity, Chernyshevsky is destined to remain worthless, unproductive in Siberia. Since work generally was not required of political prisoners, he occupies most of his time immersed in his favorite activity, reading. However, he does not turn to Pushkin, as Fyodor's father had done on his butterfly expeditions. Chernyshevsky's reading is empty. The audience, the other exiles, with whom he was occasionally blessed on a winter evening, noticed "that although he was calmly and smoothly reading a tangled tale with lots of 'scientific' digressions, he was looking at a blank notebook" (298). Chernyshevsky's fake reading is both grotesque and pathetic. The blank pages signify the emptiness of such an activity.

Fyodor proceeds to list the critic's other occupations that lead to no tangible result. Chernyshevsky's prolific writing brings him neither satisfaction nor fame, so he burns almost all of it. He also tries his hand at physical labor, but even that ends in disaster: "The pleasure which he had experienced in his youth from the orderly disposition of the St. Petersburg waters now received a late echo: from nothing to do he dug out canals—and almost flooded one of the Vilyuisk residents' favorite roads" (301). The unsuccessful canal digging shows both Chernyshevsky's inability to create anything useful and his lack of resourcefulness. He can merely copy a water system that works in St. Petersburg; he cannot invent a more suitable system for the small Siberian town. In other words, his lack of ingenuity and vision in general is the primary reason he cannot do any productive work.

One of the main reasons Chernyshevsky fails to be productive is that he remains wrapped up in a cocoon of sorts, insulated from the world and its concerns; he fails to observe the new terrain around him.[16] This disconnection is emphasized in a description of his clothing: "Suffering intolerably from drafts, he never removed either his fur-lined dressing gown or his lambskin shapka. He moved about like a leaf blown by the wind with a nervous stumbling gait, and his shrill voice could be heard now here and now there" (*G* 285). To return to the butterfly imagery used so frequently in Nabokov's works, we might think of the critic here as a sluggish larva. However, unlike a larva that eventually does shed its cocoon and turns into a beautiful free-flying butterfly, Chernyshevsky never casts off his layer of clothing. Chernyshevsky stands in contrast to Fyodor, who describes shedding his clothing in the Grünewald forest and celebrating in the warmth of the sun, which makes him feel so much a part of the forest around him that he muses that his former, pallid self is now "exiled to Yakutsk Province" (333), a noncoincidental reference to the place of Chernyshevsky's exile (see 215). Fyodor's physical unwrapping from a constrictive cocoon of clothing symbolically represents his desire to be part of his surroundings or to be expansive and free to fully explore his environment.[17]

Fyodor employs other images of entrapment to show the critic's cocooned life, pointing out that Chernyshevsky is trapped not so much by his captors as by his own eccentric habits and beliefs. For example, the portrayal of his room suggests that all the critic does is eat and sleep, that he is just a melancholy creature in a zoo. The "office" is described as "a spacious room divided by a partition; along the entire wall in the larger part there ran a low 'sleeping shelf,' in the nature of a platform; there, as if on a stage (or the way in zoos they exhibit a melancholy beast of prey among its native rocks) stood a bed and a table which were essentially the natural furnishings of his whole life" (*G* 286). Here, Fyodor's choice of vocabulary stresses Chernyshevsky's confinement: the reference to zoo indicates bars; the sleeping shelf suggests something narrow and cramped.[18] Moreover, this description of the room is more elaborate than any reference to the wider environment surrounding the civic critic. Such a limited descriptive focus exemplifies Chernyshevsky's lack of interest in exploring his natural surroundings, exemplifies his disinclination to extend his vision beyond the familiar and the known.

Fyodor reprimands the critic for such a limited outlook, for his failure to seize the opportunity to explore the Siberian countryside, and points to the punitive irony of such a situation: "He maintained with the conviction of an ignoramus that the flowers of the Siberian taiga are just the same as those which bloom all over Russia. There lurks a secret retribution in the fact that he who had constructed his philosophy on a basis of knowing the world was now placed naked and alone, amidst the bewitched, strangely luxuriant, and still incompletely described nature of northeast Siberia: an elemental, mythological punishment which had not been taken into account by his human judges" (*G* 256). Chernyshevsky's obliviousness to the natural world around him stands in stark opposition to the keen observations and discoveries of Fyodor's father, whose passion for learning about something yet unknown motivated his whole existence and serves as a model for Fyodor's own perspicacity. Chernyshevsky, however, disregards the still undescribed flora and fauna of the Siberian landscape. He merely shuttles collected flowers off to his family: "The flowers which he gathered (whose names he did not know) he wrapped in cigarette paper and sent to his son Misha" (289). This behavior is vastly different from that of Fyodor's father, who brings to a fellow scientist an entire "vegetable covering of a motley little mountain meadow in one piece, the size of a room" (114), obviously a rich scientific find.

Indeed, Chernyshevsky misses the opportunity of a lifetime because he does not explore this land. His whole experience of exile (and of life in general) can be summed up as being "blind" toward opportunities. He does not see the world around him and make the best of it. This metaphorical blindness is underscored by his literal condition of severe myopia.[19] Already, from early childhood, Chernyshevsky's eyes were noted for their "angelic clarity characteristic of nearsighted children" (*G* 212). As Fyodor comments, the child knew only those faces he kissed. Yet his first spectacles were bought only at the age of twenty. The theme of spectacles picks up again in exile, where Chernyshevsky has to resort to describing the prescription he needs in a letter to his sons by "marking the distance at which he could make out writing" (215). But in spite of his elaborate graphic efforts, "He nonetheless made a mess of it, and six months later he received from them number 'four and a half instead of five or five and a quarter'" (291). When Chernyshevsky dies, the theme of nearsightedness appears again. He is surrounded by "the dead tomes of Weber; a pair of spectacles in their case" (300), which keep getting into everybody's way, an image that perhaps foreshadows the detriment he has on future generations due to his lack of vision. As in the case of Podtyagin, whose pince-nez symbolize a lack of vision in the present that jeopardizes his ability to succeed in exile, the return to focus on Chernyshevsky's failed vision in exile emphasizes that, without a keen observation of the unfamiliar territory that an émigré confronts, exile remains a condition of unrealized dreams and a potentially deadly stasis.

Chernyshevsky's spectacles frame an extremely limited outlook, one that prevents him from productively succeeding in exile. Fyodor's outlook is much more far-reaching. He uses artistic wit, inspired in part by the lessons learned from writing about his father's perspicacity in the world of natural science, to contrast his own panoramic perspective with the limited, myopic viewpoint of the civic critic. In this way, he fashions a highly decorative work, applying his talents to make something seemingly mundane, a biography of Chernyshevsky, into an unexpectedly rich portrait. Through this sophisticated approach, he ends up releasing Chernyshevsky from a cocoon of readings based solely on ideology. Fyodor thus discovers even in this most utilitarian of writers a subject that can be creatively transformed and, along the way, finds in the tale of the civic critic's life a poignant lesson about his own present existence.

Fyodor's use of such elaborate artistry is extremely ironic, given that Chernyshevsky is the thinker most associated with utilitarianism in the Russian cultural tradition and is considered the bleakest of Russian writers (infamous for his reductive plots, unsophisticated use of language, etc.). The overt reasons behind Fyodor's choice of topic are explicitly stated in the text or become obvious throughout the reading: to cheer up his émigré friend, to approach a subject that "represents everything that Fyodor is not," to gain a distance from his personal past, and to have a "firing practice" (*G* 196).[20] Numerous critics have explored the structural and stylistic techniques Fyodor employs to accomplish these goals. The complex narrative frame structurally traps the radical thinker within its boundaries as if to keep his influence at bay.[21] And Fyodor's merciless satire, pulled off with a Gogolian flourish, both grants him an artistic distance that is lacking in his previous literary endeavor and allows him to play out a sweet revenge on this utilitarian critic who, like so many others of his ilk, scathingly attacked Gogol and others like him.[22]

However, what I explore here is what we might think of as a kind of aesthetic excess, how Fyodor's topic transcends his numerous original intentions for taking on the project. To better understand how this seemingly "utilitarian" task becomes something so beautifully patterned that it seems as if Fyodor weaves into his work an artistry and structural patterning that is reserved for him and for the "intelligent eyes" of the reader, it might be useful to recall the father's (and Nabokov's) understandings about mimicry. These ideas differ from theories that explain mimicry as a purely utilitarian mechanism, one that ensures the survival of the fittest through adaptation that allows organisms to blend into the environment to escape predators. Earlier in *The Gift*, when describing lessons learned from his father, Fyodor writes of the "incredible artistic wit of mimetic disguise," remembering that his father had stressed that it is "not explainable by the struggle for existence," that it is a natural phenomenon "too refined for the deceiving of accidental predators" and seems instead to be "invented by some waggish artist precisely for the intelligent eyes of man" (110). The critic Vladimir Alexandrov has argued that these ideas about mimicry espoused by Fyodor's father (and by Nabokov too) are close to those of the naturalist Boris Uspensky. Turning to Alexandrov's summary of Uspensky's theories can perhaps help to clarify the issues raised in *The Gift*. Uspensky rejected utilitarian theories that attempted to explain mimicry because of "the implausibility that the perfection of the mimic's imitation of a model could have been arrived at by thousands of repeated accidents" and emphasized that "the general tendency of nature is toward decorativeness, theatricalness, the tendency to be or appear different from what she really is at a given time and place . . . endless disguise, endless masquerade" (*N's O* 229).

What Fyodor accomplishes in his biography reflects his keen understanding of these lessons about mimicry, for what he achieves represents a powerful step beyond the mimetic or the utilitarian. Earlier, when writing the biography of his father, he fell victim to a kind of copying, incorporating encyclopedia accounts or failing to maintain a distance, which led him merely to follow in his father's footsteps, to merge into his father's voice and adventures. But just as his father taught him that mimicry in nature extends beyond copying to seem instead like a beautiful theatrical display, so Fyodor will find through writing his biography of Chernyshevsky that artfulness is the key to a dazzling display of his artistic wings, to a flight beyond the merely mimetic of all too many émigré writers.

Fyodor's biography thus has a much wider scope than the numerous previous biographies of Chernyshevsky had offered, biographies that were written with the purpose of furthering or cementing the civic critic's status as a cultural icon or that merely satirized the critic's failure as part of an effort to mock the father of socialist realism. By releasing Chernyshevsky from the constraints of ideological strangleholds, Fyodor grants this figure a human face, emphasizing that this man too suffered through the trials of exile. Fyodor also adds to a fuller perspective by situating the controversial figure in his time and place. By providing a humorous interplay of his relationship with many other famous Russian literary figures (Pushkin and Gogol, Leo Tolstoy and Mikhail Lermontov, to name but four), Fyodor enacts a loving tribute to the Russian literary and cultural past. This homage to an epoch and culture gone by points to the fact that, although it is outdated, it is a thing of great beauty and importance, not to be stripped of its complexities (socialist realism) or forgotten in the scurry to fashion something entirely new (the lure of exile).

Through his homage to the past and his rethinking of this cultural icon, Fyodor gains not only a more complete aesthetic education but also clearer insights into his own condition of exile. This is an understanding that he offers to his émigré audience as well; he hopes to provide readers with a new portrait of a familiar figure. The idea of a portrait is more than figurative; as Koncheyev, a fictional critic in *The Gift* (modeled in real life primarily on the poet and critic Vladislav Khodasevich), notes, many émigrés burdened themselves with a "large, framed portrait of some long-forgotten relative. Just such a portrait is for the Russian intelligentsia the image of Chernyshevsky, which was spontaneously but accidentally carried away abroad by the émigrés, together with other, more useful things. And somebody confiscated the portrait" (*G* 320).[23] Fyodor indeed confiscated the portrait for both the liberals (who idealized the critic as a sacred cow of Russian liberalism) and the conservatives (who saw him as responsible for the cultural wasteland). These émigrés have seen Chernyshevsky as if through a monocle or pince-nez, whereas Fyodor has provided a fuller perspective by concentrating on the human side of this man, especially on the very human experience that had plagued Russians for all too long, the condition of exile.

In Nabokov's novels, preserving and enriching a culture is a daunting task, but it is perhaps the most rewarding task of all. By presenting various fates of writer-intellectuals, Nabokov relates problems of cultural preservation, memory, understanding, and appropriation. An old writer's life led in poetic silence represents a disconnected personal history, which can no longer carry the burden of cultural heritage. A critic's graphomaniacal obsessions, coupled with lack of cultural knowledge and creativity, amount to no art, only tragic misappropriations of his ideas by others. The writer who does succeed must first not only gain mastery over words and subject matter but also over cultural knowledge of the past and present. Only then can he position himself in the continuum of the cultural past and thus directly be instrumental in its preservation. Nabokov is unequivocal about the power of the written word. Yet when a photograph is to assume such powers, as we will see in Kundera's presentation, ambiguity sets in.

4. Milan Kundera:
Photographers Armed and Dangerous

The Book of Laughter and Forgetting opens with Kundera's portrayal of a fateful moment in Czech history. In February 1948, Klement Gottwald stepped out on the balcony of a baroque palace in Prague to address the nation. Surrounded by his comrades, Gottwald announced the beginning of a new era, the establishment of communist Czechoslovakia. Kundera tells us that it was a cold and snowy day, that the Communist leader was hatless, and that Vladimir Clementis, standing right next to Gottwald, graciously took off his fur cap and placed it on the leader's head. Kundera goes on to explain that both the historical speech and the act of human kindness promptly became immortalized in a photograph that was subsequently disseminated by the propaganda section of the Czechoslovak Communist Party in thousands of copies. This image of a historical photograph, one of the earliest in Kundera's fiction, reveals what proves to be a topic of incessant reflection in his work: the role of photographic documentation in cultural memory.

Photography becomes the focus of Kundera's exploration of the importance of cultural memory, of the necessity of holding on to memories of the history of one's nation, as well as the rich culture one inherits. This bridge to the past is at risk when a writer is forced into exile, far from the sustenance of his native shore; it is equally jeopardized within a totalitarian regime, where questioning the versions of the past that are promoted by those in power, although dangerous, is crucial. We encounter this with the Gottwald and Clementis photograph, which, as subject to various manipulations and distortions motivated by the ever-shifting political atmosphere, keeps changing meaning and function. Initially, the photograph appears as a symbol of remembering or, more precisely, the Party's modus operandi for glorifying the depicted historical moment but also, and more important, for inscribing it on each and every individual's consciousness. This inscription of one historical moment is a synecdoche of the forceful subjugation of the entire nation to the Communist regime. To achieve this ambitious goal of shaping national consciousness, the propaganda section exploits the photograph's relatively easy reproducibility. Soon, the scene of the Communist leaders gathering on the balcony of a baroque palace appears "in hundreds of thousands of copies on posters, in schoolbooks, and museums" (*BLF* 3). In one form or another, the photo is bound to be encountered, whether it is by a child leafing through a textbook or by an adult strolling the streets of Prague. Such omnipresence, achieved by mass reproduction along with mass distribution and mass display, reveals the Party's intention to make the photograph part of the population's daily visual existence, an intention that results in the populace's inability to escape from the object itself and, by extension, from the signified Communist rule.

The photo's thorough and inescapable inclusion in the present and, by implication, future time frames is perhaps a predictable act of ideological manipulation. What does seem unexpected, however, is the photo's placement in museums, for in Czechoslovakia, photographs are exhibited in art galleries rather than in museums. Nonetheless, the photograph, which is neither ancient nor rare, is placed within the sacrosanct collection of "high" cultural artifacts, as if it can be stripped of or distanced from its context in the mundane world of day-to-day existence and ready reproducibility. It is precisely because the museum is an institution that hallows the past that the Party's intentions in placing the photograph here can be seen as both subtly refined and glaringly manipulative. In the presence of national relics and treasures, the photograph assumes exalted status deserving of honored preservation. In other words, the photograph ascends into the preserved cultural history of the nation, as if it already has historically and physically withstood the test of time.[1] Of course, beneath this attempt to imbue the photograph with the aura of a grand and significant past lies the not so well hidden absurdity that photographic technology is only a relatively recent historical development, dating from the 1830s. This absurdity is mirrored in the Czech Communist Party's attempt to rewrite its own history as deeply rooted and interminable, notwithstanding its brief existence. Despite this contradiction, the Party's success in making the photograph integral to all time frames shows a resolve to imprint both the image of the leader and the Communist regime on the collective consciousness of the nation.[2]

Ironically, soon after the photograph is used as an instrument of coerced remembering, it is suddenly manipulated so as to acquire a diametrically opposed meaning, that is, it is used as an instrument of cultural forgetting. This transformation is determined by political turmoil. We read that only four years after the birth of communist Czechoslovakia the once-solicitous Clementis standing by Gottwald on that by now famous balcony was charged with treason and hanged.[3] Henceforth, the Party's goal was quickly to eliminate Clementis from the memory of the people so that political harmony would not be questioned. And what better, easier way than to resort to photo manipulation, to airbrush the problematic figure from the original photograph, as well as from all its replicas?[4] When this aim is accomplished, the authorial voice hastily concludes the episode: "All that remains of Clementis is the cap on Gottwald's head" (*BLF* 3).

Although the unerased hat may suggest that human generosity outlives the physical existence of any single human being and that total erasure of a person is impossible, the bare palace wall— now an undisturbed blank space where Clementis once stood— suggests the ease and lure of forgetfulness.[5] Moreover, the absence created by the politically and existentially obliterated person calls for the reformulation of that fateful moment symbolizing the birth of communist Czechoslovakia, the necessity of rewriting this moment to exclude Clementis. This endeavor involves rewriting all books dealing with history, re-postering the streets of Prague, and rehanging the museums with the newly made photos. The undertaking, albeit quite elaborate, is well worth the effort to the Party. As stated later in the novel, in a dialogue between the authorial I and his friend, the well-known dissident-historian Milan Hübl, this is the most effective way not only of speeding up the process of mass forgetting but also of gaining control over a nation:[6]

> "The first step in liquidating a people," said Hübl, "is to erase its memory. Destroy its books, its culture, its history. Then have somebody write new books, manufacture a new culture, invent a new history. Before long the nation will begin to forget what it is and what it was. The world around it will forget even faster."

"What about language?"

"Why would anyone bother to take it from us? It will soon be a matter of folklore and die a natural death."

Was that hyperbole dictated by utter despair?

Or is it true that a nation cannot cross a desert of organized forgetting? (*BLF* 159)

The answer to these musings, provided by the authorial I, is nonbinding: "None of us knows what will be" (159). Such an open-ended response, as if inviting further questions, contains a glimpse of optimism, for as we know from Kundera's works, the spirit of questioning is crucial if the dogmatic agendas of totalitarian regimes are to be resisted. The images of the photographs of Gottwald, with and without Clementis, serve as just such a question, for they pose a query about history, politics, human existence, cultural memory, and photography in general.[7]

Although we may recall a few more photographs in *The Book of Laughter and Forgetting,* it is not until Kundera's next novel that he places in the thematic forefront the role of photography in cultural memory. Predictably, *The Unbearable Lightness of Being* also opens with a photographic image. This time, Adolf Hitler's portraits appear in front of the authorial narrator while he leafs through a book. What is interesting about this encounter is that the photos invoke nostalgia for the narrator's long-gone childhood rather than for the expected horror and outrage over war atrocities, which affected him personally: "I grew up during the war; several members of my family perished in Hitler's concentration camps; but what were their deaths compared with the memories of a lost period in my life, a period that would never return?" (*ULB* 4). Of course, he deems it necessary to explain the shockingly odd sensation: "This reconciliation with Hitler reveals the profound moral perversity of a world that rests essentially on the nonexistence of return, for in this world everything is pardoned in advance and therefore everything cynically permitted" (4).[8] The juxtaposition of Hitler and the theme of photography, even if only because the narrator's mention of Hitler is specifically triggered by a photo, also points to the ways in which twentieth-century totalitarian regimes often manipulate the technological possibilities inherent in photography.

The narrator connects not only photography and politics but

also photography and philosophy, establishing a link between Nietzsche's idea of eternal return and memory, specifically the role of photography in memory. This link is underscored by the close narrative proximity of the references to Nietzsche's ideas and the photograph, for the discussion of the idea of eternal return immediately precedes and follows the description of the photographic scene, as if literally creating a frame around it. In addition, the Nietzschean opening foreshadows a broader cultural setting than the one encountered in *The Book of Laughter and Forgetting,* which primarily concentrates on twentieth-century Czechoslovakia.[9] *The Unbearable Lightness of Being* moves beyond a focus on Czechoslovakia and includes ruminations on Western philosophy and has Swiss and American settings. This expansion of topic and scope also provides for a deeper and more far-reaching exploration of the subject of photography. Although in *The Book of Laughter and Forgetting* the treatment of photography is restricted to the discussion of the photograph's function, in *The Unbearable Lightness of Being* both the role of the person behind the camera and the consequences of capturing a frozen moment of reality on film are included within the purview of the narrator's panoramic gaze. These photographic issues are juxtaposed with the ongoing philosophical reflections about remembering and forgetting and are especially emphasized in the novel's pivotal scene: the scene that depicts the Soviet invasion of Czechoslovakia, a crucial event that not only motivates the main protagonists' physical and emotional upheavals but also sets the cameras clicking.[10]

The Soviet invasion of Czechoslovakia took place when the Communist Party's existence was threatened by a strong countermovement for democracy, only twenty years after the appearance of Gottwald and his cohorts on the balcony of the baroque palace. Although the countermovement seemed successful in the beginning—culminating in the Prague Spring of 1968, when euphoric freedom ruled the country, abolishing censorship, lifting bugging systems from private flats, and allowing travel abroad—it was short-lived. As Kundera puts it in terms both poetic and apt, "Russia, composer of the master fugue for the globe, could not tolerate the thought of notes taking off on their own" (*BLF* 14). On 21 August of that same year, Soviet tanks, accompanied by the Warsaw Pact forces, abruptly rolled in to crush the opposition, along with the fragile democratic movement. Unwilling to accept the rigid score of a grand fugue, in other words, the return of the totalitarian regime of hard-line communism, many Czechs fought back, especially during the first week of the Soviet occupation. Since ordinary Czech citizens were not allowed to possess weapons, they took to unconventional arms, as noted by the narrator: "young men on motorcycles racing full speed around the tanks and waving Czech flags on long staffs, . . . young girls in unbelievably short skirts provoking the miserable sexually famished Russian soldiers by kissing random passersby before their eyes" (*ULB* 67). This "carnival of hate filled with a curious (and no longer explicable) euphoria" was recorded by photographers who "were acutely aware that they were the ones who could best do the only thing left to do: preserve the face of violence for the distant future" (67).

Thus positioned in the front lines of the "battle," the Czech warriors, equipped with their ever-ready cameras and rolls of film, indeed come to represent an effective force.[11] The photographers' presence immediately creates confusion among the invading troops: "The Russians did not know what to do. They had been carefully briefed about how to behave if someone fired at them or threw stones, but they had received no directives about what to do when someone aimed a lens" (*ULB* 67). Facing the undeniable absurdity of firing bullets at the blinking shutters, the soldiers are forced to suspend their physical "activities" and resort to the mental realm in order to reach a decision on how to proceed with their battle. The need for a decision involves the challenge to the composer of the "master fugue" to risk "notes taking off on their own." But the army, temporarily immobilized and intellectually disarmed, stands powerless in front of the camera lenses.

The initial stupor is, however, quickly replaced by retaliation, a retaliation that explains why such immobility occurs. When Tereza (who is the only individually identified photographer in this novel but whose actions stand for all the other people actively documenting the invasion) takes "a close-up of an officer pointing his revolver at a group of people" (25), she is arrested and told that she will be shot at Russian military headquarters. Since the officer is never in the least bit physically endangered, the severity of his response reveals a fear of the camera, a fear of pictorial immortality. Given that the camera record has often been used as incriminating evidence, as "incontrovertible proof that a given thing happened," the thought that for all posterity one may be caught and preserved (even if only in two dimensions) in a compromising situation is psychologically forbidding.[12] What does not serve as a deterring force, however, is the real physical intimidation that Tereza faces at the hands of her captors. Immediately following her overnight detention at Russian military headquarters, she returns to the Prague streets determined more than ever to continue the unequal battle of camera lenses against tank turrets, to keep "looking danger in the face" (*ULB* 26). Although Tereza never comes to physical harm during the seven-day photographic frenzy, later, in an unrelated political event, we are reminded that documentary zeal can indeed be deadly.

Part 6, "The Grand March," depicts a protest at the Cambodian border, a "great spectacle performed before the eyes of the world" (259). This spectacle, a march consisting of "twenty doctors and about fifty intellectuals (professors, writers, diplomats, singers, actors, and mayors) as well as four hundred reporters and photographers" (259), is conducted so that a handful of Western doctors would be granted entrance into the occupied and famine-racked Cambodia. An American photographer, however, gets sidetracked from his politico-humanitarian mission by a personal whim to capture on film simultaneously both a famous Hollywood actress and a singer. "A well-known American photographer, having trouble squeezing both their faces and the flag into his viewfinder because the pole was so long, moved back a few steps into the rice field. And so it happened that he stepped on a mine. An explosion rang out, and his body, ripped to pieces, went flying through the air, raining a shower of blood on the European intellectuals" (265). On the one hand, the meaningless death during an attempt to "frame" meaningless history, along with the parodic tone used throughout this episode, underlines the ridiculousness of the entire affair. On the other hand, the scene raises important questions about what may motivate such risk-taking activity. For Tereza, these motives fall into the two oppositional categories that Kundera appropriates from Parmenides: light (gratifying a personal need) and heavy (preserving cultural history).

Both light and heavy motives influence Tereza's desire to document the Soviet invasion. On the light side, she is driven by the mundane desire for personal happiness, happiness that is possible only when jealousy is eliminated from her life. The all-consuming jealousy brought on by Tomas's infidelities leaves Tereza physically and emotionally weak. Tereza's lack of physical strength is literal: she keeps falling down or at least frequently drops objects from her shaking hands. The psychological weakness is exhibited by Tereza's feelings of suppressed, even crushed, individuality and uniqueness that result from being merely one of many women in Tomas's life. Her emotional outbursts surface, especially during the long and torturous nights, which are full of horrifyingly evocative dreams, as well as the very real smells emanating from Tomas's hair, smells that belong to other women. When the Soviet tanks roll in—significantly, at night—they suddenly and unexpectedly interrupt Tereza's nightmares and her sense of smell and replace these personal disturbances with a higher sense of meaning. Tereza suspends the unproductive jealousy and replaces it with a passionately energetic documentary activity: "The days she walked through the streets of Prague taking pictures of Russian soldiers and looking danger in the face were the best of her life. They were the only times when the television series of her dreams had been interrupted and she had enjoyed a few happy nights. The Russians had brought equilibrium to her in their tanks, and now that the carnival was over, she feared her nights again and wanted to escape them" (26–27). The camera, not Tomas, becomes Tereza's steady companion for the first seven days of the invasion. This faithful companion proves to be invaluable both historically and personally. While Tereza is framing the outer world, history in its making, she is also taking aim at an inner, personal world in which she is experiencing for the first time an unknown sense of self-worth and meaning. She catches a glimpse of a self that is independent, balanced, happy, and liberated from the pains of jealousy.[13]

In fact, Tereza uses the camera to directly confront her jealousy, aiming it at the object of her jealousy, at her husband's mistress, Sabina. Using a false pretext, she offers to take photos of Sabina and arranges a meeting. The camera provides Tereza with the necessary courage to "frame" and fulfill her unusual desire to take pictures of her husband's lover. During the women's encounter, as during the Soviet invasion, the camera comes to serve a double purpose. On the one hand, the mechanical eye offers a view of a body that Tereza desires because of her husband's desire for it, a body that she now sees in a new way because it is normally "hidden" from her; now it is no longer mysterious and unknown, no longer threatening and jealousy provoking. On the other hand, the camera provides Tereza with a "veil by which to conceal her face from [Sabina]" (*ULB* 65). This concealment from the photographed subject's view reveals Tereza's conscious protection of privacy, the hiding of her own emotional feelings. At the same time, by voyeuristically observing Sabina's body, Tereza mercilessly strips away Sabina's privacy. In essence, she appropriates the mistress's body through an optical merging with Tomas. Thus Sabina symbolically becomes a shared "plaything." We can summarize Tereza's role in this encounter by using Susan Sontag's words: "To photograph is to appropriate the thing photographed. It means putting oneself into a certain relation to the world that feels like knowledge—and, therefore, like power."[14]

Unfortunately, Tereza's newly found balance does not last long; its end corresponds to that of the "carnival," or more precisely to the seventh day of the invasion. Once Tereza sheds the double-aiming camera, her equilibrium again becomes disturbed. Desperately searching for the brief happiness she experienced while photographing, she literally escapes the feared nights by emigrating with Tomas to Switzerland. Exile, however, does not provide emotional stability; rather, it contributes to severe alienation and desperation: "Being in a foreign country means walking a tightrope high above the ground without the net afforded a person by the country where he has his family, colleagues, and friends, and where he can easily say what he has to say in a language he has known from childhood" (*ULB* 75).[15] Tereza's jealousy returns, and along with it comes the weakness from which she suffered at home; her hands again start shaking. She runs away once more, this time back to Czechoslovakia, now a country with closed borders that will never allow her to leave. Her failure to find inner balance in either country, either territory, suggests that only with camera in hand is Tereza able to gain power over her mental state.

The heavy motives behind Tereza's photographic zeal are perhaps more immediately apparent than the light motives because the heavy motives are directly connected to the historical event of the 1968 Soviet invasion of Czechoslovakia. Tereza, who openly refers to herself as prone to vertigo, clearly identifies with her nation in times of trouble: "She realized that she belonged among the weak, in the camp of the weak, in the country of the weak" (*ULB* 73). This identification or merging with centuries-old culture, language, and territory grants her the emotional strength she needs for self-sacrifice. And since a physical counterattack is inconceivable in this case, the only possible recourse is a documentary one. It is important to note that, since Tereza does not have children to whom she can pass on the results of her life-threatening activity or for whom she can try to improve the future of her country, the potential sacrifice is directed outside her personal realm. In other words, Tereza's foremost reason to fight the Soviet tanks with camera in hand is of a higher existential nature. She is motivated by a determination to preserve a fleeting moment of history and cultural memory: "All previous crimes of the Russian empire had been committed under the cover of a discreet shadow. The deportation of a million Lithuanians, the murder of hundreds of thousands of Poles, the liquidation of the Crimean Tatars remain in our memory, but no photographic documentation exists; sooner or later they will therefore be proclaimed as fabrications. Not so the 1968 invasion of Czechoslovakia, of which both stills and motion pictures are stored in archives throughout the world" (67). This quotation not only points to the photographer's special task of preservation but also blatantly privileges photography over all other means of documentation. This view reiterates the "enshrined belief in the metaphysical priority of images over words, the belief that an image directly shows us the reality which words can only communicate in a fragile and untrustworthy manner." For Tereza, who primarily communicates through dreams or dreamlike images rather than through words—"She was like her country, which stuttered, gasped for breath, could not speak" (75)—photography becomes a desirable and natural choice of expression.

Perhaps this affinity for imagery is why Tereza's photographs of the Soviet occupation are unusual, if not exceptional. Tereza's eye and talent allow her artistically to transcend the purely mechanical activity of someone hurriedly documenting a historical moment. A Swiss magazine editor refers to these photos as beautiful and marvelous, and a fellow photographer finds them especially captivating: "'Those pictures of yours, they're very interesting. I couldn't help noticing what a terrific sense of the female body you have. You know what I mean. The girls with the provocative poses!' 'The ones kissing passersby in front of the Russian tanks?'" (70). This description of Tereza's photos evokes Sabina's paintings, in which "incongruous things came together: a steelworks construction site superimposed on a kerosene lamp; an old-fashioned lamp with a painted-glass shade shattered into tiny splinters and rising up over a desolate landscape of marshland" (101). Similarly, Tereza's images involve the incongruity of fragile women's bodies juxtaposed with the massive tanks. We recall that Sabina, in fact, was a mentor to Tereza, who listened "with the remarkable concentration that few professors ever see on the face of a student" (63). Sabina learned about pictorial art during the height of socialist realism, when strict mimetic faithfulness was required of everyone. At that time, Sabina "had tried to be stricter than her teachers and had painted in a style concealing the brush strokes and closely resembling color photography" (63). As Sabina explains, her self-imposed strictness quickly dissipated once she dripped some paint on one of her photographic paintings by mistake. The trickle of paint, like a crack, reveals another, less known world: "On the surface, an intelligible lie; underneath, the unintelligible truth" (63). The "double exposures," the "confluence of two themes," and the knife slicing at the backdrop to reveal the truth epitomize Sabina's artistic vision.[16] Tereza appropriates this vision in her photographic endeavor, as can be seen from the above-mentioned photo revealing the juxtaposition of the Russian tanks with young, miniskirted Czech women kissing passersby, thus disturbingly titillating the sexually famished Russian soldiers. The soldiers positioned in their massive tanks, of course, also violate the space of the women and the invaded country, which these women so provocatively defend.[17] It is important that Tereza never resorts to doctoring or manipulating her photos to achieve the double-exposed effect. She captures reality as is with her artistic eye, searching "behind the scenes," unveiling the truth. This striving for truth is also represented in the handing over of most of her undeveloped rolls of film to Westerners, who can immediately smuggle them out of the country. She does not want to beautify or reconstruct the pictures or choose the best of them. Her photos are meant to furnish evidence; they are not to be tampered with but are to portray history as it happened. Thus, unlike the propaganda section of the Communist Party described in *The Book of Laughter and Forgetting,* which was busy airbrushing persons from photographs and thus rewriting history, Tereza does not even wait to see how most of her photos turn out.

But what role do these photographs play once smuggled across the Czech border? We are told that some (not necessarily Tereza's) immediately appear in well-known magazines. This initial popularity is short-lived, however. When Tomas and Tereza find themselves in exile, a few weeks following the occupation, Tereza tries to place the few photos she developed herself in a Swiss journal, as an attempt to keep her birth nation alive abroad. Ironically, these pictures that represent the potential to preserve Czech cultural memory fail to do so when presented in the West. The Swiss editor certainly appreciates the photographs' quality but is no longer interested in the politics of Czechoslovakia, even when Tereza objects that nothing is yet over in Prague. The West is in the process of forgetting the Soviet invasion, already preoccupied with the next calamitous historical event. This comment on the short attention span of the West is satirized in *The Book of Laughter and Forgetting:* "The bloody massacre in Bangladesh quickly covered over the memory of the Russian invasion of Czechoslovakia, the assassination of [Salvador] Allende drowned out the groans of Bangladesh, the war in the Sinai Desert made people forget Allende, the Cambodian massacre made people forget Sinai, and so on and so forth until ultimately everyone lets everything be forgotten" (*BLF* 7). Once taken outside the borders of their homeland, these photos become part of a long chain of forgetting, one of many quickly flashing images of world historical events, none of which is remembered for long. In a Western context where safety and freedom are not immediately jeopardized, the initial shocking impact of these photos quickly fades. Stripped of their context and meaning, their life span is even shorter than that of the political event they happen to depict.

The phenomenon of brisk forgetting is consciously embarrassing to the Swiss editor. Uncomfortable in front of Tereza, the editor is grateful for the distraction of a colleague's sudden entrance. This professional photographer momentarily diverts attention from politics by showing her photos of nudists to Tereza. When the two women photographers are introduced and proceed to examine each other's work, Tereza makes an odd, cryptic comment about how her photos of the occupation are similar to those of the nudists. Thus she indirectly returns to the subject of politics.

> "Have a look at mine in the meantime," she said.
> Tereza leaned over to the folder and took out the pictures.
> Almost apologetically the editor said to Tereza, "Of course they're completely different from your pictures."
> "Not at all," said Tereza. "They are the same."
> Neither the editor nor the photographer understood her, and even I find it difficult to explain what she had in mind when she compared a nude beach to the Russian invasion. (*ULB* 69)

Tereza's mysterious analogy and the lack of comprehension among those present, including the narrator, are perplexing.[18] Nonetheless, comparison with a scene in *The Book of Laughter and Forgetting* suggests possible links between violence, nudity, and totalitarianism. The passage is worth quoting in full.

> They went naked down the steps to the beach, where other naked people were sitting in groups, taking walks, and swimming—naked mothers and naked children, naked grandmothers and naked grandchildren, the naked young and the naked elderly. There were naked breasts galore, in all shapes and sizes—beautiful, less beautiful, ugly, gigantic, shriveled. Jan came to the melancholy conclusion that not only did old breasts look no younger next to young ones but equally bizarre and meaningless.
> And once again he was overwhelmed by the vague and mysterious idea of the border. Suddenly he felt he was at the line, crossing it. He was overwhelmed by a strange feeling of affliction, and from the haze of that affliction came an even stranger thought: that the Jews had filed into Hitler's gas chambers naked and en masse. He couldn't quite understand why that image kept coming back to him or what it was trying to tell him. Perhaps that the Jews had also been *on the other side of the border* and that nudity is the uniform of the other side. That nudity is a shroud. (*BLF* 226)

These two disturbing scenes—one in which Tereza suggests

that there is no difference between her photos of violence and the photos of nude bodies; and the other, in which nude bodies evoke the horrors of the gas chambers—both emphasize a theme that emerges frequently in Kundera's works: that the naked body can represent a frightening reduction of human existence to an indistinguishable uniformity. A naked body is one stripped of what makes a human being an individual. If existence is limited to the merely physical, the beauty of the soul can be too easily obliterated.[19] Tereza is acutely aware of this tendency; haunted by her mother's shameless parade of nakedness, which made a mockery of privacy, she is also constantly disturbed by Tomas's infidelities, which to her equate her body with those of all others, denying the uniqueness of her soul. This fear emerges in her nightmares, which often depict a terrifying reduction of the human body to an object of repressive control:

> While she marched around the pool naked with a large group of other naked women, Tomas stood over them in a basket hanging from the pool's arched roof, shouting at them, making them sing and do kneebends. The moment one of them did a faulty kneebend, he would shoot her.
>
> Let me return to this dream. Its horror did not begin with Tomas' first pistol shot; it was horrifying from the outset. Marching naked in formation with a group of naked women was for Tereza the quintessential image of horror. (*ULB* 57)

Perhaps Tereza ascertains a similarity between her photos and the nude photos because, to her, they both document the stripping away or obliteration of unique identities: hers record the erasure of Czech cultural memory under the Soviet invasion, while the others depict nude bodies reduced to exchangeable art objects, without individuality or soul.[20]

Tereza's photos regain a more pointed political relevance when she returns to her homeland, followed by Tomas, replacing exile with the totalitarian regime of Czechoslovakia. In a perverse twist of fate, these documents of violence against a helpless people now serve to implicate not those who committed the violence but those who were its victims. In other words, the Communists, regaining their power, exploit the photos published in Western magazines to implicate those Czechs opposing the Soviet invasion and Communist rule. Tereza now sees her role

differently: "How naive they had been, thinking they were risk-
ing their lives for their country when in fact they were helping the
Russian police" (*ULB* 142). Thus the once history preserving
photograph is now the corpus delicti to be used against the active roles played by both the photographers and their subjects in
subverting the Communist regime. As undesirable elements in the
reestablished communist society, they are soon eliminated from
active life, from their jobs and posts, and, by extension, from the
memory of others. They are erased from history, if not from life,
as Clementis was twenty years prior to the Soviet invasion.

The different meanings that accrue to the invasion photographs recall the opposing readings of the famous photograph
described in the opening of *The Book of Laughter and Forgetting*.
After Kundera's emphasis on the importance of Clementis's
gesture of lending his hat to the cold and hatless Gottwald, it may
come as a surprise to discover that, as Jindřich Toman notes,
Kundera in fact made up the whole hat episode. In 1989, the
Czech journal *Kmen* once again reproduced the original photograph depicting the birth of communist Czechoslovakia. Here
Gottwald appears in a fur cap, and right next to him stands the
smiling Clementis sporting an elegant hat. It does not appear as
if anybody is giving away anything at all, or that Clementis ever
possessed a fur cap.[21] True, the unfortunate Clementis was erased
four years later from this photograph, but so was his elegant hat.
Why Kundera's roguish play with the reader? Have we been
manipulated? At whom is this event directed? The implied readers surely are not restricted to the minuscule Czech émigré audience, who would know the author's fictionalization of this
event. Is this a private "joke" on the Western reader between
Kundera and his few fellow Czechs? Have we believed and privileged a photographic image and a narrative account over cultural
memory, over memories passed down from those who witnessed
the scene on the balcony? I would argue that Kundera is not leading us astray but warning us against our own tendencies toward
forgetfulness and acceptance of the written and printed word as
if it were a photo, thus requiring no further questioning. Just as
Eduardo Cadava suggests "that the most faithful photograph,
the photograph most faithful to the event of the photograph, is
the least faithful one, the least mimetic one—the photograph that
remains faithful to its own infidelity," so Kundera remains faithful to infidelity, refusing to encourage or allow the reader to settle

into the comforting half-truths of an unquestioning mimetism.[22] The seductive danger of taking photographs at face value is also emphasized by Sontag, who points out that photography "implies that we know about the world—but this is the opposite of understanding, which starts from not accepting the world as it looks."[23] Like Sabina, who through her paintings discovers or reveals a truer world beyond superficial appearances, we are urged through Kundera's manipulation of the theme of photography in *The Unbearable Lightness of Being* and *The Book of Laughter and Forgetting* to look behind the scenes, to question what is all too often taken for granted, and thus, as Sontag suggests, to move a bit closer to understanding.

The questioning of what is truth and what is not truth, a questioning that is crucial if cultural memory is to be preserved against a totalitarian imposition of willed forgetfulness, is emphasized through the thematic exploration of photography in *The Unbearable Lightness of Being* and, more broadly, through this work's form as a novel. Just as the Czech photographers, armed with cameras, battle the Russian soldiers in a struggle against the erasure of Czech identity and cultural memory, erasures that will surely occur under the Soviet takeover, so too do Kundera's theory of the novel and his practice of writing in this genre struggle against the threat of its possible obliteration under the totalitarian art agenda. In recent critical discussions, Kundera has become one of the most often quoted proponents of the idea that one of the key generic requirements of the novel as a form is that it be a vehicle for questioning. As Kundera puts it, "Totalitarian Truth excludes relativity, doubt, questioning; it can never accommodate what I would call the *spirit of the novel.*"[24]

Kundera reacts specifically against the thousands of formulaic and programmatic "novels" published in huge editions and mandatorily read in the former Soviet and Eastern bloc countries.[25] As he says: "These novels add nothing to the conquest of being. They discover no new segment of existence; they only confirm what has already been said; furthermore: in confirming what everyone says (what everyone must say), they fail to participate in the *sequence of discoveries* that for me constitutes the history of the novel; they place themselves *outside* that history, or if you like: they are *novels that come after the history of the novel.*"[26] *The Unbearable Lightness of Being,* with its incessant questioning, is

a response to the disruption of this history. It showcases the art
of questioning both to criticize narratives that refuse to do so and
to participate in the sequence of discoveries that constitutes the
history of the novel, thus restoring a bridge or continuity between this novel and the great novels of the world's cultural past.

Ironically, Kundera's *Unbearable Lightness of Being* has been read
as a novel with a closed and resolved ending by critics who interpret the final chapter as optimistic, happy. These critics may
be led astray by Tomas's last words to Tereza, words that suggest
that inner peace and freedom may be found in their last escape
or exile, on a cooperative farm in the Czech countryside: "And
it's a terrific relief to realize you're free, free of all missions" (313).
Susan Moore, for example, claims that while living in the country, Tomas and Tereza find fulfillment and peace of mind: "No
one envies them; no one interferes with them—certainly not the
Red Army or the police; and no one threatens their freedom of
speech or movement."[27] Catherine Fellows, in her analysis of
Kaufman's film adaptation of *The Unbearable Lightness of Being*,
points out, "As we watch the couple herding cows on a screen
framed by trees and mist, we could be looking at an old master:
there is no mistaking this for 'objective reality.'"[28] This comment
suggests that the rosy depiction of life in the country is too good
to be true, but Fellows goes on to argue that the end of the film,
and of the novel, offers us a vision of some kind of mythic resolution of opposites, as if the rural scenes depict some great "circle of life": "The screen is dominated by the growing of crops,
the care of livestock, the preparation of meals, the healing of
the injured arm, by dancing and spontaneity. Maybe here is the
centuries-old narrative framework in which the lightness of being is made bearable by the weight of time; in which even death
can be accommodated."[29]

However, I argue that both Moore and Fellows (in her comments on Kaufman's film version) are too optimistic in their
interpretations. The country idyll described by Kundera is like a
photograph, a surface, and one needs to look *through* it. In fact,
a close look at the entire final section, entitled "Karenin's Smile,"
reveals that happiness is undermined in several ways: the chapter is infused with a melancholy mood, which is brought about
by the death of animals; the bucolic life is described as machine-
like; and the poorly maintained machines of this supposed paradise turn out to be responsible for the deaths of Tomas and

Tereza. In addition, because the deaths of these two have already been mentioned and described earlier in the novel, an ominous tone pervades the entire chapter, playing on our awareness that they will soon be killed.

Although the final chapter does not contain the actual deaths of Tomas and Tereza, it includes other deaths that force the protagonists to confront their own mortality. The dog, Karenin, has cancer and must be put to sleep; Tereza dreams of Tomas's death by shooting (which results in his metamorphosis into a rabbit), and the narrator recalls the extermination of pigeons in Prague and the campaigns against dogs that were meant to divert attention from the Soviet invasion. Also, the word *smrt* (death) and its verbal or adjectival cognates appear twelve times in this relatively short chapter (thirty pages in the original). These seemingly unimportant deaths and the frequent repetition of the word *smrt* create a melancholy tone, create an ending that is far more unsettling than unequivocally happy.[30]

A happy ending is also undermined in the descriptions of the people and animals of the rural communal farm: they are machinelike, stripped of their individuality and freedom. The machines themselves are poorly cared for; we know that the brakes of Tomas and Tereza's old truck will give way and result in their deaths. We learn that "the villages were turned into a large collective factory, and the cows began spending all their lives in the five square feet set aside for them in their cow sheds. From that time on, they have had no names and [have] become mere *machinae animatae*" (*ULB* 290). A farmer "who no longer owns his own land and is merely a laborer tilling the soil" (283) no longer has reason to care about the land or the work he does. He becomes apathetic, encloses himself in the four walls of his dwelling (like the cow in its shed), and stares "at the refulgent television screen." Although people in the country have nothing to lose or fear and have therefore maintained a certain amount of autonomy (for example, they can choose their own collective farm chairman), they are far from free. Tomas cannot practice medicine, nor can he or Tereza go anywhere else because they have sold all their possessions to move here. Their deaths are due to negligence, which reveals the true conditions of this supposed paradise: "The police determined later that the brakes were in disastrous condition" (123). Thus the collective farm does not symbolize a new and better life; it is permeated by death, and its inhabitants are automatons, struggling to make ends meet with machines and on a farm in which few invest care.

In addition to these thematic emphases on death, the structural technique of achronology, one of the key narrative techniques used to promote open-endedness and a spirit of relentless questioning in *The Unbearable Lightness of Being,* adds to the ominous tone.[31] The actual death scene is presented as an analepsis, appearing in the middle of the novel where it makes little sense, in a section devoted to Sabina and the misunderstandings she faces in emigration. Furthermore, the death scene is followed by four more parts that deal directly or indirectly with Tomas's life. In other words, the reader is told that Tomas dies on a collective farm before, according to the plot chronology, he actually moves there from Prague. To place the death scene of the main protagonist so early in the text seems anticlimactic. Why does the narrator opt for this deliberate chronological displacement?

By revealing the conclusion of the novel much earlier than the reader expects, the narrator eliminates suspense and "lays bare" his technique with all its complexities. When a text is dominated by a suspenseful plot, the reader can block out everything but the outcome of the novel. This early mention of the novel's outcome creates the expectation in the reader's mind of a death scene; at the same time, it reveals the climax of the story and eliminates suspense. The reader no longer needs to question what will happen, only how and when. Kundera frustrates our expectations of a "happily ever after" ending in which answers would be provided and problems solved; instead, it leaves much open to question (for example, Did Tereza's love finally win out? Did Tomas become weak at the end? Did the totalitarian system succeed in eliminating all freedom from this society?).

Kundera's questioning form is analogous to Sabina's aesthetic, which she describes as similar to a knife that slices through the surface to reveal deeper or contradictory truths below.[32] Kundera's art of questioning, like his thematic foregrounding of characters who constantly question, slices through the superficial picture promoted in a totalitarian agenda, a picture that obliterates not only a cultural past but also a narrative tradition characterized by questioning. Kundera puts it best:

> The novel's spirit is the spirit of complexity. Every novel says to the reader: "Things are not as simple as you

think." That is the novel's eternal truth, but it grows steadily harder to hear amid the din of easy, quick answers that come faster than the question and block it off. In the spirit of our time, it's either Anna or Karenin who is right, and the ancient wisdom of Cervantes, telling us about the difficulty of knowing and the elusiveness of truth, seems cumbersome and useless.

The novel's spirit is the spirit of continuity: each work is an answer to preceding ones, each work contains all the previous experience of the novel. But the spirit of our time is firmly focused on a present that is so expansive and profuse that it shoves the past off our horizon and reduces time to the present moment only. Within this system the novel is no longer a work (a thing made to last, to connect the past with the future) but one current event among many, a gesture with no tomorrow.[33]

A photograph is a figure of knowledge. Knowledge comes only in flashes, in a moment that is both illuminating and blinding. This duality, stated first by Walter Benjamin, is inherently Kundera's. In *The Book of Laughter and Forgetting* and *The Unbearable Lightness of Being,* photography plays an ambiguous role to say the least. We see photographers document historical and cultural moments; but at the same time, they unknowingly implicate people for "treason." We are presented with a photo that ought to capture a moment for posterity yet is doctored, and a new image, which looks just as authentic as the old, creates memory anew. We are led to understand that a camera is used as a documentary tool; nonetheless, its lens turns into a weapon. At the end, only paradoxical questions remain. Can a photograph preserve or document a cultural or historical moment? Do we in our present privilege images over words? Kundera offers one noncommittal answer and that is to return to the wisdom of Cervantes.

Conclusion: *The Art of the Novel*

Kundera laments the lost history or tradition of the novel, which has led to the loss of "the ancient wisdom of Cervantes . . . about the difficulty of knowing and the elusiveness of truth."[1] To get at what he suggests here, a turn to Franz Kafka, as in the introduction, yields a provocative starting point. In a parable entitled "The Truth about Sancho Panza," Kafka offers a strange scenario about the playful elusiveness of truth according to this wisdom:

THE TRUTH ABOUT SANCHO PANZA

Without making any boast of it Sancho Panza succeeded in the course of years, by feeding him a great number of romances of chivalry and adventure in the evening and night hours, in so diverting from himself his demon, whom he later called Don Quixote, that this demon thereupon set out, uninhibited, on the maddest exploits, which, however, for the lack of preordained object, which should have been Sancho Panza himself, harmed nobody. A free man, Sancho Panza philosophically followed Don Quixote on his crusades, perhaps out of a sense of responsibility, and had of them a great and edifying entertainment to the end of his days.[2]

In Kafka's retelling of the journeys of Miguel de Cervantes's famous pair, he imagines a reversal of roles, in which Sancho is creator and Don Quixote, rather than an initiator of adventures, is a demon exorcised from and by Sancho. This scenario is puzzling indeed, as are so many of Kafka's parables and other writings. But what is of interest here is how this scenario suggests the ways in which a successful émigré writer expels his or her demons, as well as how this exorcism is assisted by a return to the "ancient wisdom" embodied in the history of the novel.

To see the connection between Sancho's creativity in this parable and the task any writer faces as he or she sits down to shape experience and imagination into fiction, we need to focus on Sancho's role as storyteller. Troubled by a demon, Sancho feeds the demon stories, romances of chivalry and adventure, in the evening and night hours (a time suggestive of the haunting of dreams and memories). Through the telling of these stories, Sancho is able to divert what haunts him, to separate a perhaps debilitating demon from himself. He identifies and names his demon and sets him off on what becomes a marvelous journey without "preordained" destination—although the victim or target would have otherwise been Sancho. Because of the distance between Sancho and his demon created through the exorcism, the former is able to follow from a bemused and philosophical perspective. The crusades thus become "a great and edifying entertainment," journeys both pleasurable and enlightening that encompass enjoyment *and* responsibility.

The émigré writers Nabokov and Kundera, like Sancho, successfully divert their demons, thus turning a potential nightmare of painful exile into extraordinary literary journeys. The demons troubling these writers are those that haunt the treacherous terrain of exile: a possible fall into meaninglessness (weightlessness) if the past is entirely forgotten (the fate of Sabina in Kundera's *Unbearable Lightness of Being*); a desperate sense of loss, which follows a mistaken insistence on a too literal recuperation of the past (which plagues Tamina in *The Book of Laughter and Forgetting*); or a deadly stasis, which occurs when one disregards the potential that the present offers (as does Podtyagin in Nabokov's *Mary*). What a successful émigré writer must do is exorcise the potentially dangerous tendencies of memory by fashioning an imaginative combination of past and present, shape the art of memory in exile—as the fictional writer Fyodor does in *The Gift*, and as Nabokov and Kundera do. Indeed, both writers weave their novels out of their experience and knowledge of both shores and cultures, out of words both native and natively appropriated, out of a fusion of the past and present. To accomplish this is to escape another kind of demon, the burden of feeling victimized by a political regime or, alternatively, by the new cultural environment in which an émigré must make his or her way. These writers are not held hostage by their pasts; they find in them something personally and culturally enriching, something that is unique and unknown in the new environment. Rather than dwell on their own victimization or exploit that of others, they shoulder the past with a strong sense of responsibility.[3] To exorcise the potentially devastating effects of a demonic possession by the past in such ways is to be free; like Sancho's Don Quixote, the demons are let out into a creative space full of possibilities.

This creative space is one fostered in the vast tradition of the novel. Kundera, evoking Nabokov with his lepidopteral imagery, talks about a time when the novel was in flight: "Rabelais' time was fortunate: the novel as butterfly is taking flight, carrying the shreds of the chrysalis on its back."[4] It was an extraordinary time, in which all was possible, even Gargantua's birth from his mother's ear.[5] Unfurled was the plausible with the implausible, "allegory, satire, giants and ordinary men, anecdotes, meditations, voyages real and fantastic, scholarly disputes, digressions of pure verbal virtuosity."[6] Having experienced a time that was far less extraordinary—a private and public history of fracture and outrage, of strictest artistic control and censorship—Kundera and Nabokov yearn for that ever-elusive freedom. They locate a world full of possibilities (private and public) not only on the shores of exile but within their own aesthetic. This aesthetic is woven out of the usual threads of boundless imagination, life experience, and stylistic forte, but additionally and distinctly, it is embellished by proud memory. It is precisely memory, a possession that was carried off to and shaped by exile, that allows for an unexpectedly unique voice to emerge, a voice that explores and expands the possibilities of the novel form.

At first glance, the voices of the two writers do not seem to have much in common. Nabokov's style is so intricately and seductively rich that it may never cease to interest the literary critic. The endlessly winding sentences, the unexpected turns of individual words, the implausibly playful images, the exquisite verbal games are just a few features that create an unprecedented linguistic mosaic. Nabokov's love affair with words, old and newly created, native and natively appropriated, offers a challenge to translator and reader alike. Kundera, on the other hand, does not burden the literary critic with stylistic innovations, puzzles, or games. He works his style into an art of elegant simplicity and stark precision, an art of "tongue-tied eloquence," to borrow Barańczak's term. Worried about mistranslation, his texts contain painstaking explanations of precise meanings of individual words, embedded dictionaries with elaborate descriptions of concepts, and imagery devoid of excessive poeticism to avoid ambiguity.[7] Kundera weighs heavily every word against another, pondering all of its implications not only in Czech but in other languages as well.[8]

Nonetheless, these seemingly disparate styles, one explosive, the other restrained, share a common stylistic tactic that, as a product of their exilic imagination, is at the heart of their aesthetics. The tactic demands the activation of a reader's memory through the process of textual decipherment. In Nabokov's works, the burden on the reader is great because the author, mirroring the workings of mimicry, utilizes a strategy of deception through concealment. Alexandrov explains how this maneuver works: Nabokov's texts consist of "numerous, intimately interwoven strands of motifs (relating to physical objects, colors, shapes, states of mind, literary allusions, etc.), the component elements of which are often concealed by being placed in unrelated contexts, or by being alluded to in an understated and oblique manner" (*N'sO* 14). Thus the tactic challenges the reader's memory either "to accumulate the components of a given series, or to discover the one detail that acts as the 'key' for it; when this is achieved, the significance of the entire preceding concealed chain or network is retroactively illuminated" (7). Nabokov realizes the difficulty of this task and offers the reader a model for an interpretive strategy through his characters, who also "are involved in trying to make sense of some of the same details that confront the reader, and often dramatize what appear to be plausible conclusions about them" (14). Predictably, because Kundera is not imitating the "artistry" of the Lepidoptera, his stylistic tactic is more overtly visible, although the demands on the reader's memory and interpretative abilities are the same. The tactic is based on iteration. Images, motifs, sentences, even entire scenes, are repeated, at times verbatim, throughout the text. Naturally, the compulsion is to retrieve the repetitions and then compare and contrast them. This compulsion is strengthened by the narrator's frequent allusions to the repetitions, which not only underline their presence but bring the reader to an awareness of the importance of carrying the past forward as one reads. The present and future time of reading thereby becomes richer, denser, and more meaningful. Ultimately, as the whole work becomes illuminated through the repetitions, the reader is brought to a new awareness through his or her own recall.

The stylistic tactic, with its implied process of decipherment imposed on the reader—either through the discovery of connections among details and motifs or through the retrieval of repetitions—has important implications. Alexandrov enumerates these implications for the reader of Nabokov; arguably the same hold true for Kundera: "Since the conclusion that the reader makes depends on his retaining details in his memory, he appears to have an atemporal insight into some aspect of the text's meaning; he is thus lifted out of the localized, linear, and temporally bound reading process" (*N'sO* 7). This process of reading, Alexandrov continues, is satisfying because it allows for hidden meanings in the text to emerge and is also seductive, for it "creates the illusion of verisimilitude by allowing the reader to function as in 'real life'" (14). In other words, the accumulation of textual clues, which in turn may illuminate the overall meaning of the text, is a much more satisfying and "real" experience than a reading that does not demand decipherment.[9] It is our own art of retention, our own accumulation of flashes, snippets, details, that entice our imagination. Roland Barthes's ideas on reading reiterate the same thoughts: "The pleasure of the text is not the pleasure of the corporeal striptease." Rather, it is "intermittence, as psychoanalysis has so rightly stated, which is erotic: the intermittence of skin flashing between two articles of clothing (trousers and sweater), between two edges (the open-necked shirt, the glove and the sleeve); it is this flash itself which seduces, or rather: the staging of an appearance-as-disappearance."[10]

To evoke Barthes here is not only to restate that pleasure is evoked through the reader's own imaginative decipherment of a detail, a tear or edge (to use Barthes's terms), but also to underscore Nabokov's and Kundera's desire to "seduce." To entice the reader is every writer's goal, yet this compulsion is more vital, more urgent for a writer in exile than for a writer who is on home ground. The exilic writer is uniquely positioned, faced with two audiences, the fellow exiles and the readers of the newly adopted country; he has to fashion a voice that would lure both. The new readers who are not familiar with the experience of exile may be enticed by the theme alone.[11] The intricate stylistic tactic offers an additional level of satisfaction. If, however, this level goes unnoticed (which it very well may), the text still retains something of the newly encountered and thus remains enticing. The exilic audience, on the other hand, has the "privilege" of personally knowing the textual theme. The trials, tribulations, and triumphs of exile are their very own. The pleasure of reading about one's own experiences is comforting but short-lived. The émigré needs to have his or her imagination challenged, and thus a stylistic tactic based on decipherment can offer satisfaction from the unknown, the unpredictable.

In addition to evoking the reader's pleasure, the process of decipherment challenges the reader to "see" better. Because the narrative flow is nonlinear—interrupted by the reader's search and accumulation of motifs, details, and repetitions—alertness, or cognitive engagement, becomes an integral part of the reading process.[12] As a result, the reader's sense of perspicacity and of independently gained understanding is increased. Of course, an integral part of the process of "seeing" better is memory, which due to the text's interrupted flow is challenged. To piece together narrative fragments, to determine meaning, the reader has to go back as he or she moves forward, to retrieve and recall. Put to the test here is not only the reader's memory but also his or her patience, since the end is inevitably delayed. The slowness that inevitably accompanies a reading based on decipherment results in heightened retention. Thus the emphasis is not only on recalling events from the past but on retaining them and carrying them into the future. The stylistic maneuver mirrors the theme that memory and vision are crucial and that the past has to be carried forward.

The emphasis on memory is not surprising. All writers of exile, as already discussed, are excessively absorbed with its workings. However, Nabokov and Kundera take an additional step: they bring the reader actively into the process of evoking, restraining, forming, and shaping memory. They share with their reader a privileged space of knowledge and creation. The reader becomes part of an act of preservation. Personal, cultural, historical moments are remembered not only through the text but also through the reader's participatory memory. In a sense, the reader is challenged to greater humanity, humanity that calls for independence, remembrance, perspicacity, understanding, imagination, and will.[13]

By responding to their exilic condition through the creation of such a style, of such adventuresome works, Nabokov and Kundera gain the freedom to access a tradition that propels the novel to take flight, to rise above any ideological or utilitarian purpose. Like certain butterflies, which according to Nabokov display a kind of theatrically playful mimicry that extends beyond what seems necessary for survival, the narratives of these two writers appear to be "invented by some waggish artist precisely for the intelligent eyes of man" (*G* 110). By appropriating and experimenting with the rich structural, thematic, and stylistic play exhibited in the history of the novel, the exilic fictions of these writers create a bridge to this wider history of the novel, crossing "kingdoms," so to speak, creating vistas to imagined worlds where all again becomes possible.

These imagined worlds come to full view in Nabokov's and Kundera's narrative works that follow their respective explorations of the terra firma of exile. Having exorcised their exilic demons, having crossed over spatial, linguistic, and cultural abysses, having explored the possibilities of memory on both thematic and stylistic levels (especially in *The Gift* and *The Unbearable Lightness of Being*), the authors gained and realized the freedom to explore worlds in which, according to Kundera, "bridges and the filler have no reason to be and in which the novelist would never be forced—for the sake of form and its dictates—to stray by even a single line from what he cares about, what fascinates him."[14] *Lolita, Ada, Immortality,* and *Slowness,* to name a few, are novels of complete aesthetic and creative utopia, novels in which imagined worlds are based on superimposed territories (America and Russia in *Ada*), time fluidity (eighteen and twentieth centuries in *Slowness*), thoroughly individualistic cultural submersion *(Lolita, Immortality),* and an elaborate game of linguistic hopscotch *(Lolita, Ada).* Although these works are truly extraterritorial, creating kingdoms that transcend physical and national boundaries, they are firmly anchored within the tradition of the novel, the very tradition that György Lukács called the form of "transcendental homelessness."

Postscript

Kundera lives in a time when physical return to his former homeland is possible. One may ask, Why has he not returned to the "place to which his imagination, his obsessions, and thus his fundamental themes are bound"?[1] He provides an answer via novelist Witold Gombrowicz's refusal to see Poland again, reasons Kundera calls existential and incommunicable, "Incommunicable because too intimate. Incommunicable, also, because too wounding for others. Some things we can only leave unsaid."[2]

Notes
Bibliography
Index

Notes

INTRODUCTION: *OTHER SHORES*

1. Franz Kafka, *The Complete Stories,* ed. Nahum N. Glatzer (New York: Schocken Books, 1971), 411–12.
2. See Clayton Koelb, "The Turn of the Trope: Kafka's 'Die Brucke,'" *Modern Austrian Literature* 22, no. 1 (1989): esp. 63–64, on the ambiguity of bridge and body. For a discussion of *The Metamorphosis* along these lines, see Stanley Corngold, "Kafka's *Die Verwandlung:* Metamorphosis of the Metaphor," *Mosaic* 3 (summer 1970): 91–106.
3. Milan Kundera, *The Unbearable Lightness of Being,* trans. Michael Henry Heim (New York: Harper and Row, 1984), 75; hereafter cited in the text as *ULB.*
4. Michael Seidel, *Exile and the Narrative Imagination* (New Haven: Yale University Press, 1986), 4; hereafter cited in the text as *ENI.* Split between the two shores, an émigré inevitably becomes divided, doubled, or twinned, or in Joseph Conrad's words, a "homo duplex." See Joseph Conrad, *A Personal Record: The Works of Joseph Conrad* (London: Dent Uniform Edition, 1946), 121.
5. The various problems encountered in exile are explored, for example, by Elizabeth Klosty Beaujour, *Alien Tongues* (Ithaca: Cornell University Press, 1989); Paul Tabori, *The Anatomy of Exile: A Semantic and Historical Study* (London: Harrap, 1972); Julia Kristeva, "A New Type of Intellectual: The Dissident," in *The Kristeva Reader,* ed. T. Moi (Oxford: Blackwell, 1986); and the collected essays by exiles in Marc Robinson, ed., *Altogether Elsewhere: Writers on Exile* (New York: Harcourt Brace, 1994); hereafter cited in the text as *AE.*
6. In his novel *Ada,* Vladimir Nabokov constructs a territory called Amerussia. It consists of two worlds that magically merge together, creating an exilic idyll. For more on this, see Seidel's discussion of *Ada* (164–74).
7. Joseph Brodsky, "The Condition We Call Exile," *Altogether Elsewhere: Writers on Exile,* ed. Marc Robinson, 3–11.
8. Edward Said, "The Mind of Winter: Reflection on Life in Exile," *Harper's,* September 1984, 54; hereafter cited in the text as *MW.*
9. Henri Bergson, *Creative Evolution,* trans. Arthur Mitchell (New York: University Press of America, 1983), 200, states, "As long as we regard the past as merely past we impoverish our present."
10. Koelb, 58, points out that this image of an impassable height relates to the idea of the elevated heights that figurative language can reach.

11. See Ruth V. Gross's sexual interpretation of the passerby and the bridge in "Fallen Bridge, Fallen Woman, Fallen Text," *Newsletter of the Kafka Society of America* 5, no. 1 (1981): 15–24. Also note Koelb's ideas (see 61, 62, 65).

12. Gleb Struve sees these possibilities as positive; he emphasizes that there is no need to exaggerate the uprootedness of exilic literature, that, in fact, its advantage is to be sought in the freedom that it enjoys: "Emigration is a great evil, but enslavement is a much greater one." See Struve, "Russian Writers in Exile: Problems of an Émigré Literature," *Comparative Literature* 2 (1958): 603.

13. As David Bethea, *Joseph Brodsky and the Creation of Exile* (Princeton: Princeton University Press, 1995), 39–40, points out,

    > The Russian context offers countless examples of this very contrapuntal thinking; it is particularly foregrounded among the so-called first wave of émigré writers who wrote for dwindling audiences in Berlin and Paris during the interwar period. Vladislav Khodasevich, for example, says virtually the same thing as Said but does so poetically, in his marvelous poema (narrative poem) *Sorrento Photographs,* where the photographic negative of life in revolutionary Russia shows through, as in a double exposure on the snapshots of life in and around Gorky's villa near Sorrento.

14. Also see Bethea, *Joseph Brodsky,* 39. To romanticize the notion of exile is to mute its tragic tongue-tie and to turn it, inevitably, into something compensatory—an "enabling fiction" that permits the artist "to transform the figure of rupture back into a 'figure of connection'" (*ENI* x, xii).

15. See Stanisław Barańczak, "Tongue-Tied Eloquence: Notes on Language, Exile, and Writing," in *Altogether Elsewhere: Writers on Exile,* ed. Marc Robinson, 242–51, for a discussion of various translation problems encountered in exile.

16. Vassily Aksyonov, "Lungs and Gills," in *Altogether Elsewhere: Writers on Exile,* ed. Marc Robinson, 234.

17. Breyten Breytenbach, "A Letter from Exile, to Don Espejuelo," in *Altogether Elsewhere: Writers on Exile,* ed. Marc Robinson, 16.

18. Eva Hoffman, "Obsessed with Words," in *Altogether Elsewhere: Writers on Exile,* ed. Marc Robinson, 231. Her optimism is almost impossible among older writers who have no prior language of their adopted country.

19. Svetlana Boym, "Estrangement as a Lifestyle: Shklovsky and Brodsky," in *Exile and Creativity: Signposts, Travelers, Outsiders, Backward Glances,* ed. Susan Rubin Suleiman (Durham: Duke University Press, 1998), 244, states: "A portable home away from home, which an émigré ferociously guards, preserves an imprint of his or her cultural motherland."

20. Stanley Kubrick's *Lolita* and Philip Kaufman's *Unbearable Lightness of Being* have been enormously successful.

21. The kaleidoscope is described as a simple optical instrument that, although sold as an amusing toy, has "real value for the pattern designer and offers an admirable illustration of the image-forming properties of combined inclined mirrors" (*Encyclopedia Britannica,* 15th ed., s.v. "kaleidoscope"). Nabokov and Kundera can be viewed as novelistic pattern designers.

22. Nabokov and Kundera treat their pasts in diametrically opposed manners. Nabokov wrote a detailed autobiography and provided personal and artistic material to his biographers. Kundera, on the other hand, discusses little of his past, rarely grants interviews, and even "erases" from his oeuvre some of his earlier works—poetry and drama.

23. Moreover, the weaving of culturally based recollections into a work of fiction fulfills a preservation function, for it resists both individual forgetting and deliberate erasing or rewriting by the regime that expelled its writer.

1. Vladimir Nabokov: *Variations on a Butterfly*

1. Vladimir Nabokov, *Mary,* trans. Michael Glenny with the collaboration of the author (New York: Vintage International, 1989), 5; hereafter cited in the text as *M.*

2. Brian Boyd, *Vladimir Nabokov: The Russian Years* (Princeton: Princeton University Press, 1990), 246; hereafter cited in the text as *VN:RY.*

3. Nabokov and many other Russian émigrés left their country via boat. Thus the drawer, "as deep as a ship's hold" (*M* 6), is an emblem of personal memory in transit.

4. Leona Toker, *Nabokov: The Mystery of Literary Structures* (Ithaca: Cornell University Press, 1989), 43–44, asserts that Mary's ambiguous photographic presentation is indicative of the novelist's critical attitude toward Ganin.

5. Henri Bergson, *Matter and Memory* (New York: Zone Books, 1988), 82–83.

6. Julian W. Connolly, *Nabokov's Early Fiction: Patterns of Self and Other* (Cambridge: Cambridge University Press, 1992), 38; hereafter cited in the text as *N's EF.*

7. Bergson, *Matter and Memory,* 133–34. For a study of how the presentation of memory in *Mary* is influenced by Bergson's philosophy, see Eric Laursen, "Memory in Nabokov's *Mary,*" *Russian Review* 55, no. 1 (1996): 55–64.

8. Connolly, 32, makes a similar observation: "While one part of Ganin—his consciousness—inhabits a cerebral realm of memory, his physical body continues to inhabit a Berlin pension."

9. John Burt Foster Jr., *Nabokov's Art of Memory and European Modernism* (Princeton: Princeton University Press, 1993), notes that delays are part of Ganin's creative technique; Mary does not become part of his memories until much later (see esp. 56).

10. See Laursen, note 31.

11.   Kundera, in his novel *Slowness,* trans. Linda Asher (New York: Harper Collins, 1996), presents the idea of slowing down the time of lovemaking by imposing form, by dividing the night into three stages, for only then can the event be committed to memory. He states that "there is a secret bond between slowness and memory, between speed and forgetting" (39).

12.   See chapter 3 for a full discussion of Podtyagin's problems in exile.

13.   Klara's repetitive existence in exile reminds one of Tamina's (from Kundera's *Book of Laughter and Forgetting*) life in the West. See chapter 2 for more on Tamina's fate.

14.   Ganin does not dwell on failures of his memory. His past (unlike Tamina's) does not have to be re-created precisely to the last detail.

15.   Toker, 44.

16.   Joann Karges, *Nabokov's Lepidoptera: Genres and Genera* (Ann Arbor: Ardis, 1985), 21–22, notes that, in *Mary,* the few references to butterflies are primarily used as similes. In addition to the Camberwell Beauty, Karges points to Frau Dorn's dog, with its "pendulous ears that had velvety ends like the fringes of a butterfly's wing" (6). To return to the Camberwell Beauty, known in the United States as the Morning Cloak, Karges traces its appearance in several of Nabokov's other works, such as *The Real Life of Sebastian Knight* and *Speak, Memory,* where the image "symbolizes love, but an evanescent love" through its velvety wings (31).

17.   This image of Mary as a rare butterfly, occasionally fluttering in front of Ganin's eyes not only describes her but is symptomatic of the entire affair. Their relationship consists of episodes that are loosely tied together, disconnected due to frequent relocations, separations, and even lack of interest.

18.   In Kundera's *Unbearable Lightness of Being,* Sabina brings a seemingly useless bowler hat with her into exile, for it is a reminder of her personal past. See chapter 2 for further discussion.

19.   Karges, 22, discusses a parallel occurrence in *Speak, Memory,* where Tamara's letters "would search for a fugitive address and weakly flap about like bewildered butterflies set loose in an alien zone, at the wrong altitude, among unfamiliar flora" (Nabokov, *Speak, Memory* [New York: G. P. Putnam's Sons, 1966], 251).

20.   Nabokov had no other choice; the Russia he once knew had vanished under the Stalinist regime, and no return journey was possible without dire consequences. Martin Edelweiss, an émigré hero from Nabokov's novel *Glory,* does return to Russia. The outcome of his return is fatal, as implied in the conclusion of that novel.

21.   Boyd, 465–66, reads this scene as paying tribute to Nikolay Gogol's *Dead Souls.* He notes that the Lorentzes, so minutely described by Fyodor, prove to be irrelevant to the rest of the novel. Their irrelevant role reminds the reader of the two muzhiks discussed in great detail in the opening scene of Gogol's *Dead Souls,* also never seen again in the course of the novel. See also Nabokov's critical work *Nikolay Gogol* (Norfolk: New Directions, 1944).

22. Vladimir Nabokov, *The Gift,* trans. Michael Scammel with the collaboration of the author (New York: Vintage International, 1991), 9; hereafter cited in the text as *G.*

23. Toker notices that all of Fyodor's literary attempts are in various stages of incompleteness. For more on the motif of fragments in *The Gift,* see Toker, esp. 148–50.

24. See Sergei Davydov's discussion of how "Fyodor's development as an artist loosely parallels the path of the history of Russian literature of the nineteenth century" in "*The Gift:* Nabokov's Aesthetic Exorcism of Chernyshevskii," *Canadian-American Slavic Studies* 19, no. 3 (1985): esp. 359–60.

25. Fyodor's transformation of a patterned wallpaper into a "distant steppe" recalls Ganin's transformation of a patterned wallpaper into people's profiles. Each marks the creative approach toward his past.

26. Vladimir E. Alexandrov, *Nabokov's Otherworld* (Princeton: Princeton University Press, 1991), 119, points out that, in this scene, Fyodor's artistic imagination is described "in terms of travel imagery, which is of course his father's domain"; hereafter cited in the text as *N'sO.*

27. The influence of Pushkin on Fyodor's artistic development has received much critical attention. See, for example, Sergei Davydov, "Weighing Nabokov's *Gift* on Pushkin's Scales," in *Cultural Mythologies of Russian Modernism: From the Golden Age to the Silver Age,* ed. Boris Gasparov, Robert P. Hughes, and Irina Paperno (Berkeley: University of California Press, 1992), 415–28; and Monika Greenleaf, "Fathers, Sons, and Impostors: Pushkin's Trace in *The Gift,*" *Slavic Review* 53 (spring 1994): 140–58.

28. See Boyd, 461–64, on the subject of fate in this novel.

29. Stephen Jan Parker, *Understanding Vladimir Nabokov* (Columbia: University of South Carolina Press, 1987), 59, notes that Fyodor cherishes these lessons and examples by his father, whom he rarely saw, because he taught him how to see, "how to bring 'knowledge-amplified love' to the act of observation, a talent which is indispensable to a writer."

30. Alexandrov (*N'sO* 118) points out that "the relation between Fyodor's father and the ideal form of perspicacity that Nabokov describes in 'The Art of Literature and Commonsense' is perhaps the closest in his entire fictional oeuvre."

31. Karges, 39, traces and then interprets the lepidopteral imagery throughout Fyodor's reminiscences about his father as a way of finding out about the father's "double life," perhaps even a second family somewhere in China or Tibet.

32. In fact, some Arctic butterflies appear only once in every two years because the warm season is too brief for them to complete their full-fledged growth in one year. This phenomenon, however, was not known until after the 1940s. Thus, to Nabokov, who was writing *The Gift* in the 1930s, the once-in-two-years appearance of the Black Ringlet butterfly was indeed mysterious. I am grateful to Dr. Lawrence Gilbert of the Zoology Department at the University of

Texas at Austin and Dr. Robert Robbins of the Smithsonian Institution National Museum of Natural History for sharing this information with me.

33. Nabokov's contribution to the study of the Blue butterfly is dealt with in Kurt Johnson and Steve Coates, *Nabokov's Blues: The Scientific Odyssey of a Literary Genius* (Cambridge: Zoland Books, 1999).

34. David Bethea, "Style," in *The Garland Companion to Vladimir Nabokov*, ed. Vladimir E. Alexandrov (New York: Garland, 1995), discusses this passage in terms of style. He also warns that one should be "careful not to read too much into such passages, but there is the temptation to see the strong caterpillar-become-exotic Blue as a kind of Sirin substitute (*sirin* itself being a rara avis): the hoi polloi are not allowed, thanks to the great artist's protective coloration, to get 'at him,' to paw him with their dirty limbs, to prey on him with their ant-hill psychology" (700).

35. I owe this observation to Marjorie E. Rhine and Ronald Harris, both of Southeastern Louisiana University.

36. I thank Dr. Naomi Pierce of the Harvard Museum of Natural Sciences for this information.

37. Alexandrov (*N's O* 227) states that "the high degree of congruence between Nabokov's formulations and those of [Petr] Uspenski and [Nikolai] Evreinov is what suggests that his thinking about mimicry may have been derived from, or at least influenced by them."

38. Michael Begnal, "Fiction, Biography, History: Nabokov's *The Gift*," *Journal of Narrative Techniques* 10, no. 2 (1980): 140.

39. As Begnal, 141, asserts, the biography of his father, in essence, helps Fyodor to "free himself from the net of the past" and to "step outside himself so that his own 'I' can assimilate the essence of Chernyshevski."

40. Here Karges, 36–39, also alludes to the father's double life with a mistress, even a second family.

41. Fyodor adds a few of his personal comments to the encyclopedia entry. Yet I would argue that this personal touch is minimal and insignificant because it does not lead to any artistry, as can be seen from the following example: "A love of lepidoptera was inculcated into him by his German tutor. (By the way: what has happened to those originals who used to teach natural history to Russian children—green net, tin box on a sling, hat stuck with pinned butterflies, long, learned nose, candid eyes behind spectacles—where are they all, where are their frail skeletons—or was this a special breed of Germans, for export to Russia, or am I not looking properly?)" (*G* 102).

42. D. Barton Johnson, in *Worlds in Regression: Some Novels of Vladimir Nabokov* (Ann Arbor: Ardis, 1985), 185, notes that this passage, according to Vera Nabokov, sets forth the principal theme of Nabokov's writing—a theme termed "potustoronnost'," or the hereafter.

43. See Connolly, 203, for more on how this transformation occurs.

44. Several lepidopterists have told me that observing the Blue butterfly emerging from the anthill in a natural setting is an extremely trying and difficult task.

45. Fyodor sees that "the verbal creation of proximate worlds cannot literally be offered as a simple substitute for or copy of reality itself" (Roger B. Salomon, *"The Gift:* Nabokov's Portrait of the Artist," in *Critical Essays on Vladimir Nabokov,* ed. Phyllis A. Roth [Boston: G. K. Hall, 1984], 193).

46. The reason Fyodor abandons the biography is provided in the text. While tracing the last memories of his father, Fyodor recalls his father's favorite Kirghiz fairy tale. This tale is worth retelling in full, for it summarizes the importance of vision, which Fyodor lost during the process of writing his father's biography:

   The only son of a great khan, having lost his way during a hunt (thus begin the best fairy tales and thus end the best lives), caught sight among the trees of something sparkling. Coming closer he saw it was a girl gathering brushwood, in a dress made of fish-scales; however, he could not decide what precisely was sparkling so much, the girl's face or her clothing. Going with her to her old mother, the young prince offered to give her as bride-money a nugget of gold the size of a horse's head. "No," said the girl, "but here, take this tiny bag—it's little bigger than a thimble as you can see—go and fill it." The prince, laughing ("Not even one," he said, "will go in"), threw in a coin, threw in another, a third, and then all that he had with him. Extremely puzzled, he went off to consult his father.

   > All his treasures gathering,
   > public funds and everything,
   > in the bag the good khan threw;
   > shook, and listened, shook anew;
   > threw in twice as much again:
   > just a dingle in the drain!

   They summoned the old woman. "That," she said, "is a human eye—it wants to encompass everything in the world"; then she took a pinch of earth and filled up the bag immediately. (*G* 147)

   The prince's lack of perspicacity mirrors Fyodor's, who loses a balance between the imaginary and the real. Parker, 60, sees the moral of this tale in that: "The eye is an all devouring organ and there is immeasurably more wealth to be obtained (observed) in nature than to be found in worldly riches. The natural world—that is, 'reality,'— closely and lovingly observed, endlessly revealing, holds the greatest wealth, and thus the artist, like the scientist, in this most fundamental sense is a realist mining an inexhaustible lode."

47. Salomon, 185. For more on the subject of how Fyodor becomes the author of the novel, see Sergei Davydov, *"Teksty-Matreshki" Vladimira*

Nabokova (München: Verlag Otto Sagner, 1982), 188–99. On the structure of the novel, see Irina Paperno, "Kak sdelan *'Dar'* Nabokova," *Novoe Literaturnoe Obozrenie* 5 (1993): 138–55; and Alexander Dolinin, *"The Gift,"* in *The Garland Companion to Vladimir Nabokov,* ed. Vladimir E. Alexandrov, 135–65.

48. Yasha's biography and the poem for Zina are two other examples of Fyodor's literary endeavors but are not of consequence in this discussion.

49. See Davydov, *"Teksty-Matreshki,"* 183–99; and Toker, 160–62.

50. According to Nabokov, *Nikolay Gogol,* 149, circles are always vicious.

51. Philip Sicker, "Practicing Nostalgia: Time and Memory in Nabokov's Early Russian Fiction," *Studies in 20th Century Literature* 11, no. 2 (1987): 254.

2. MILAN KUNDERA: *VARIATIONS ON LETTERS AND BOWLER HATS*

1. Milan Kundera, *The Book of Laughter and Forgetting,* trans. Michael Henry Heim (New York: Harper and Row, 1984), 165; hereafter cited in the text as *BLF.*

2. This is not to suggest that she should rewrite her life, only that she should approach it more creatively. In Kundera's world, keeping meticulous and literal accounts of daily existence, although a way of battling personal forgetting, is presented negatively. In the first part of *The Book of Laughter and Forgetting,* Mirek's diaries, full of careful notes documenting discussions of current political situations, result not in the preservation of memory but in the politically motivated imprisonment of his son and friends.

3. As the narrator describes, the diaries are left behind in Czechoslovakia because, had they been discovered at the border during a routine customs check, Tamina and her husband would have fallen under suspicion of illegally leaving the country. For who would carry an entire archive of their private life to the sea for a two-week vacation? Of course, Tamina and her husband were planning their emigration very carefully; the repercussions of being found guilty of illegal departure were tremendous. Of all the possible places to keep her diaries safe, Tamina chooses a desk drawer. This hiding place is poignantly appropriate, for it evokes self-censorship. East European and Russian authors who were censored for political reasons used the expression "to write for a desk drawer" to imply that their work would not be officially published or read. Tamina undergoes self-censorship not because her diaries possess politically unacceptable content but because their personal meaning is so dear to her that she cannot bear having anyone read them.

4. Maria Němcová Banerjee sees Tamina's quest to recall the past through the exercise of disciplined memory as a quixotic journey turned inward. See Banerjee, *Terminal Paradox: The Novels of Milan Kundera* (New York: Grove Weidenfeld, 1990), 146; hereafter cited in the text as *TP.*

5. I find it interesting to note that the reader never gains access to the

diaries, so the reader's gaze never becomes despoiling and intrusive, never analogous to the gaze of the mother-in-law.

6. Readers might protest that this possibility jeopardizes their understanding of this book. In Kundera's fiction, Czech historical events are explained sometimes even in great detail, but discussions concerning the culture are either absent or cryptic—relegated instead to the author's essays.

7. Eva Le Grand, *Kundera; or, The Memory of Desire,* trans. Lin Burman (Waterloo: Wilfrid Laurier University Press, 1999), notes that *The Book of Laughter and Forgetting* unleashed a polemic regarding its genre. Can it be referred to as a novel when only two of the seven parts are linked by the same character (Tamina), while the other five parts deal with protagonists who are not linked together at all? Le Grand argues that indeed it is a novel, for its coherence rests on thematic unity, and its composition is based on "serial repetition" (73–74).

8. Fred Misurella, *Understanding Milan Kundera: Public Events, Private Affairs* (Columbia: University of South Carolina Press, 1993), 38; hereafter cited in the text as *UMK.*

9. See Misurella's discussion, 39, of the various parallels between the Book of Tobit and *The Book of Laughter and Forgetting.*

10. Bruce M. Metzger, ed., *The Apocrypha of the Old Testament* (New York: Oxford University Press, 1965), 63.

11. John O'Brien, *Milan Kundera and Feminism* (New York: St. Martin's, 1995), 101, interprets the Raphael in jeans as the demonic counterpart of Madame Raphael; hereafter cited in the text as *MKF.*

12. This slide is surely a literalization of metaphor à la Kafka; it is no coincidence that Kafka is mentioned in the opening section of this part. I thank Marjorie E. Rhine for pointing out this allusion to me.

13. For more on this subject, see Hana Píchová and Marjorie E. Rhine, "Kundera's Kafka and Kafka's Kundera," *Modern Czech Studies* 11 (1999): 65–73.

14. For Kundera, a world dominated by children is the ultimate trap. See Květoslav Chvatík, *Svět románů Milana Kundery* (Brno: Atlantis, 1994), esp. 85, for more on this subject.

15. The meaninglessness of sex evoked in this scene brings to mind the bragging man on television who combines all his life's orgasms into one.

16. O'Brien (*MKF* 102) notes that this choice of an escape route signals Tamina's desire to reach "a middle space outside the territorial waters of the oppositional forces that have dominated her life, she would rather drown than return to one or the other shore."

17. See Banerjee, 176–84, for a discussion of Tamina's and Kundera's fathers' death scenes.

18. The discussion about Sabina's bowler hat is presented in my article "The Bowler Hat as a Monument to Time Past in Milan Kundera's *The Unbearable Lightness of Being,*" 14, no. 2 (1997): 5–19. In *The Book of Laughter and Forgetting,* a fur cap is tied to the theme of memory and forgetting, as well as to rewriting the past. See chapter 4 for a thorough discussion of the cap's meaning.

19. Colette Lindroth, "Mirrors of the Mind: Kaufman Conquers Kun-

dera," *Film-Literature Quarterly* 19, no. 4 (1991), 233, also links the hat's ambiguity to the idea of eternal return: "The black derby, redolent of formality, propriety, convention, does indeed suggest the past, but, since it now belongs to Sabina, as free and womanly as the hat is conventional and masculine, it suggests at the same time how much that past has changed. Since there is no eternal return, the wearers of the hat, and the world they represent, are gone forever. The hat, and Sabina, are here today."

20. Identifying two types of repetition, J. Hillis Miller, *Fiction and Repetition* (Cambridge, Mass.: Harvard University Press, 1982), distinguishes between the Platonic and the Nietzschean types. The former is "based on genuine participative similarity or even on identity" (6). The children's island in *The Book of Laughter and Forgetting* comes to mind. The latter emphasizes change and instability; it "posits a world based on difference" (6). Against the background of the Nietzschean repetition arises the ever-changing image of the bowler hat.

21. The translator preserves the repetition from the Czech original in which *význam*, "meaning," reverberates five times.

22. Fred Miller Robinson, "The History and Significance of the Bowler Hat: Chaplin, Laurel and Hardy, Beckett, Magritte, and Kundera," *Tri-Quarterly* 66 (spring–summer 1986): 173–200, esp. 197.

23. Robinson, "History and Significance," 197.

24. As Robinson, "History and Significance," 197, points out: "When the bowler is light, the contrast it makes with Sabina's nakedness and lingerie is comic and erotic, 'a sign of her originality.' Yet the opposition can suddenly signify violence 'against her dignity as a woman . . . humiliation,' and the 'hard masculine hat' becomes heavy (pp. 86–87)."

25. My reading of the bowler hat differs from that of O'Brien (*MKF* 115), who claims that the hat "does not signify lightness once and weight some other time, pivoting from one either/or extreme to the other."

26. O'Brien (*MKF* 114) sees Franz's failure to comprehend Sabina here as an inability "to conceive of the hat as an expression of the tension of opposites," in other words, an inability to view the world in paradoxes. Unlike Tomas, who himself is torn by opposites and thus can appreciate the hat, Franz pursues only clear interpretations.

27. Tamina's silence about cultural differences comes to mind here.

28. Bergson, *Creative Evolution*, 200–201.

29. See Nina Pelikan Straus, "Erasing History and Deconstructing the Text: Milan Kundera's *The Book of Laughter and Forgetting*," *Critique: Studies in Modern Fiction* 28 (1987): 79.

30. In fact, many of Kundera's characters have a conflict between past and present. In his first novel, *The Joke,* the main protagonist ob-sesses so much over the past that it takes over his entire present existence.

31. *The Book of Laughter and Forgetting* does not lend itself to this discussion because of its extreme fragmentation. For more on the role of the narrator in *The Unbearable Lightness of Being,* see Hana Píchová, "The Narrator in Milan Kundera's *The Unbearable Lightness of Being*," *Slavic and East European Journal* 36, no. 2 (1992): 217–26.

32. Milan Kundera, *Art of the Novel*, trans. Linda Asher (New York: Grove, 1988), 86, states that the seven-part "structure doesn't represent some superstitious flirtation with magical numbers, or any rational calculation, but a deep, unconscious, incomprehensible drive." Le Grand, 40–41, makes a provocative link between Kundera's *Art of the Novel* and his first seven novels. She suggests that there may exist

> a secret link between the seven parts of his essay and his seven novels. It is not mere chance that the semantics of the interplay between illusion and reality in *Laughable Loves* corresponds to the thought on the playfulness of Cervantes. Or that the *Book of Laughter and Forgetting* (his fifth) evokes the same memoryless world as Kafka's, as does chapter five of *The Art of the Novel;* that the "Seventy-one words" of chapter six of the essay find a formal and semantic echo in the "words misunderstood" of *The Unbearable Lightness of Being,* that *Immortality,* the seventh and latest of his novels, as well as part seven of *The Art of the Novel[,]* evoke, each in its own way, the struggle between kitsch and the novel of which [Hermann] Broch spoke.

33. *The Book of Laughter and Forgetting* also repeats two of the chapter titles. For further comments relating to the structure of this novel, see Herbert Eagle, "Genre and Paradigm in Milan Kundera's *The Book of Laughter and Forgetting,*" in *In Honor of Ladislav Matějka,* ed. Lubomír Doležel (Ann Arbor: University of Michigan Press, 1984), 251–84.

34. Gérard Genette, *Narrative Discourse: An Essay in Method,* trans. Jane E. Lewin (Ithaca: Cornell University Press, 1980), 113–14, distinguishes among four types of narrative frequencies: a narrative may tell once what happened once, n times what happened n times, n times what happened once, once what happened n times. I will concern myself only with the third type: narrating n times what happened once.

35. Kundera, *Art of the Novel,* 147, defends repetition as a technique for achieving a certain purpose and effect: "I reject the very notion of synonym: each word has its own meaning and is semantically irreplaceable."

36. Genette, 54.

37. Wolfgang Iser, "The Reading Process: A Phenomenological Approach," in *Reader-Response Criticism,* ed. Jane P. Tompkins (Baltimore: Johns Hopkins University Press, 1980), 50–70, esp. 62–63. Here Iser discusses the act of re-creating the text as a necessary process for the reader. The process of re-creation involves looking forward, backward, making decisions, then changing these decisions, forming expectations, questioning, accepting, and rejecting. This process is directed by two structural components within the text: first, by a repertoire of familiar literary patterns and recurrent literary themes with allusions to familiar social and historical contexts; second, by a technique to set the familiar against the unfamiliar. Elements of the

repertoire are backgrounded or foregrounded with either overmagnification or trivialization, at times even annihilation of the allusion. This defamiliarization of what the reader thought he or she recognized creates a tension and intensifies his or her expectations, as well as his or her distrust of these expectations.

38. Shlomith Rimmon-Kenan, *Narrative Fiction: Contemporary Poetics* (London: Routledge, 1989), 122.

3. VLADIMIR NABOKOV: *WRITERS BLIND AND DANGEROUS*

1. See Bethea, *Joseph Brodsky*, 44.
2. For more on émigré publishing, see Marc Raeff, *Russia Abroad: A Cultural History of the Russian Emigration, 1919–1939* (Oxford: Oxford University Press, 1990), 86.
3. Connolly, 32, notices that Klara is pining away for Ganin, Ganin is dreaming of Mary, and one of the male dancers is so bored that he makes an advance at Ganin. Of course, all of these desires remain unfulfilled.
4. I thank Ronald Harris for this insight.
5. Kierkegaard's analogy of two neighboring kingdoms, discussed in the introduction, could be recalled here. For a typical émigré, the kingdom once so familiar, the homeland, is now relegated to the imaginary, is no longer so familiar, whereas the new country of exile, previously only imagined, becomes (necessarily so) very real.
6. In Kundera's *Book of Laughter and Forgetting,* Tamina literally falls silent following her inability to deal with the present situation of exile. For more on this subject, see chapter 2.
7. Although we have seen that Ganin's frequent recalls of Russia and of his love affair have a liberating effect, his recollections were carefully constructed and planned in order to enrich the present condition. Podtyagin, however, is unable to make use of or pattern his reveries into a whole; consequently, memories remain merely fragmented, disturbing.
8. Laursen, 60.
9. Not surprisingly, many of Nabokov's literary critics have posed the same question. Chernyshevsky's biography, which occupies chapter 4 of *The Gift,* is considered one of Nabokov's most polemical writings. In 1937, the editors of the journal *Sovremennye Zapiski* omitted the entire fourth chapter from their publication of *The Gift.* Nabokov's "sacrilegious" portrayal of Chernyshevsky had offended the socialist revolutionaries who at that time dominated the editorial board of that journal. In the novel itself, Fyodor predicts both negative reviews and rejections of Chernyshevsky's biography. Nabokov comments on the censorship in his foreword: "a pretty example of life finding itself obliged to imitate the very art it condemns" (1). In 1952, *The Gift* was finally published in its entirety.
10. For more on the role of Pushkin in this novel, see Davydov, "Weighing Nabokov's *Gift*," 419; and G. M. Hyde, *Vladimir Nabokov: America's Russian Novelist* (London: Marion Boyars, 1977), 17–34.

11. Davydov, *"The Gift,"* 358.

12. Davydov, *"The Gift,"* 358.

13. Much has been written about Chernyshevsky's portrayal by Fyodor, specifically, How consistent is the fictional presentation with historical facts? See, for example, Paperno; and Davydov, *"The Gift"* and "Weighing Nabokov's *Gift*."

14. Chernyshevsky was exiled to penal servitude in Siberia because of his literary activities on the journal the *Contemporary.* Fyodor elaborates that Chernyshevsky's activities represent writings that "turned into a voluptuous mockery of the censorship" (*G* 276) that ruled Russia at the time. Fyodor admires and values his protagonist's stubborn fight against censorship, as can be seen from Fyodor's satirical portrayal of the censorship department: "The authorities were fearful, for example, lest 'musical notes should conceal anti-governmental writings in code' (and so commissioned well-paid experts to decode them)" (276).

15. Chernyshevsky's lack of observation and interest is, of course, in opposition to the father's or to Fyodor's, who finds himself in the contrapuntal environment of Berlin and remembrances of Russia.

16. The weather is to blame for Chernyshevsky's lack of interest in a previous journey, one to England. According to Fyodor, such a potentially fascinating journey should have been cherished by the critic and extensively written about. He points out that the critic was extremely interested in both the country and its culture (embodied for him by Charles Dickens and the *Times*). However, the trip turned out to be unmemorable and short, consisting only of four days in London. "Chernyshevsky never spoke of his journey and whenever anyone really pressed him, he would reply briefly: 'Well, what's there to talk about—there was the fog, the ship rocked, what else could there be?'" (273). In addition, Fyodor accentuates the critic's obliviousness by obscuring the trip in the biography. He devotes very little narrative time—only one page—to the journey to reflect what few impressions it had left on his character.

17. In chapter 1, see my discussion of Fyodor turning into a butterfly, spreading out his artistic wings. Fyodor's artistry allows him to free himself from the constraints of exile and to flourish as a successful writer, reveling in the stunning patterns and designs of his work.

18. Nabokov uses bars as a symbol of imprisonment in his other novels as well. In *Luzhin's Defense,* a chessboard evokes bars. The chess player Luzhin becomes so obsessed with the game that he loses free will and finally commits suicide. In *Invitation to a Beheading,* prison bars separate the protagonist, Cincinnatus, from the rest of the world. However, since Cincinnatus never loses his identity and free will he does eventually gain his freedom not only from his prison cell but also from the two-dimensional fictional world.

19. Chernyshevsky's lack of vision is evident especially in the literary realm. As Fyodor points out, the civic critic spends his time writing and burning his work. Only the *Prologue* and a few stories and a cycle

of unfinished novellas are preserved (*G* 290). Then he spends most of his time translating "with machine-like steadiness volume after volume of Georg Weber's *Universal History*" (294). Yet this futile venture—it had already been translated by E. Korsh—shows an inability for creative thought in exile. He is reduced to a machine that only produces something that has already been done.

20. Begnal, 140.

21. Fyodor encloses the biography within two halves of a split, inverted sonnet. These two parts create a circle, and because the two stanzas placed at the end of the biography are actually the first stanzas of the poem, the reader is compelled to go back to the first page of the biography to read the final two stanzas. The end thus takes the reader to the beginning again and again, ad infinitum, ironically a kind of perpetual-motion machine from which Chernyshevsky never escapes. According to Simon Karlinsky, Nabokov's short story "Krug" has the same circular structure as Chernyshevsky's biography. See Karlinsky, "Theme and Structure in Vladimir Nabokov's 'Krug,'" in *Russian Literature and American Critics*, ed. Kenneth N. Brostrom (Ann Arbor: Department of Slavic Languages and Literatures, 1984), 243–47.

22. According to Begnal, 141, "In writing this biography, Fyodor has turned his greatest weakness into his greatest strength—he has allowed his intrusive 'I,' which caused so much trouble with his father's story, freedom to deal with Chernyshevski." Davydov, *"The Gift,"* 359, notes that chapter 3 of the novel details Fyodor's "Gogol' period," in which Fyodor learns to detect "poshlust" and sees that Gogol's use of the grotesque displays how "poshlust" can be mocked though style. He not only writes about Chernyshevsky's life to show the ridiculousness of his ideas but also uses Gogolian techniques of humor to exact a sweet revenge for the misappropriation of Gogol by materialist critics. See Hyde, esp. 17–34.

23. Hyde, 24, argues that Fyodor replaces the old portrait with a new picture, "one in which art breathes life into dry bones." And in fact, Chernyshevsky does come to life not as a sacred icon or as a hero but as a human being. Ultimately, the civic critic receives unexpected freedom from the idolized image that was at odds with his real human identity.

4. MILAN KUNDERA: *PHOTOGRAPHERS ARMED AND DANGEROUS*

1. To place the photograph in the museum is to restore to it an "aura," which, as Eduardo Cadava notes, is typically undermined by the photograph's "capacity for reproduction and circulation." Furthermore, recalling Walter Benjamin, Cadava states that the easy replication of "any given negative an indefinite number of times" disconnects the artwork from "the history of a tradition that has always privileged the artwork's uniqueness." In other words, photographs (as well as film), rather than being defined by their "cultic value" as works of art, are now being characterized by their "exhibitional

value, by the ability to circulate and be exhibited" (Eduardo Cadava, "Words of Light: Theses on the Photography of History," *Diacritics* 22, nos. 3–4 [1992]: 93, 94). Ironically, the Communists' manipulation of this particular photo and its effects manages to overcome the loss of aura in "the age of mechanical reproduction": it serves as widely distributed and politically useful propaganda and yet retains its cult value. See Katerina Clark's discussion of these phenomena in Soviet literature in Clark, *The Soviet Novel: History as Ritual* (Chicago: University of Chicago Press, 1981), 40.

2. Cadava again comes to mind: "If politics, however, fascist no less than communist, depend on photography and film's capacity to exhibit and manipulate bodies and faces, then all politics can be viewed as a politics of art, as the technical reproduction of an image" (97).

3. The marked speed in which a political figure falls into disfavor is stylistically reflected by Kundera's fast-paced narration.

4. The manipulation of photography is as old as photography itself. See Roland Barthes, *Image-Music-Text*, trans. Stephen Heath (New York: Hill and Wang, 1977), 21, on the effectiveness of photographic tricks: "The methodological interest of trick effects is that they intervene without warning in the plane of denotation, they utilize the special credibility of the photograph—this, as was seen, being simply its exceptional power of denotation—in order to pass off as merely denoted a message which is in reality heavily connoted; in no other treatment does connotation assume so completely the 'objective' mask of denotation."

5. Misurella, 44, sees Clementis's hat as a positive symbol because it keeps reappearing throughout the text:

It is almost as if Vladimir Clementis's hat is a fictional character with a mind of its own and, aware it sits on the wrong head in the famous touched-up photograph, now seeks its proper owner. Leaving Papa Clevis's head (he is too naive, too fashionably avant-garde politically), it flies to the dead humanist in his grave and provokes chaotic laughter (the laughter of the Devil) in solemn circumstances. At the orgy, on the other hand, the hat is portrayed in its exaggerated absence, the bald man calling to mind Clementis, who was airbrushed out of Czech history after 1948. The hat represents character, intelligence, and presence in the human world. By a nice ironic turn it also represents a form of human hope, a reminder that even in the bleakest circumstances, something, no matter how small and ridiculous, remains of the human spirit.

6. Milan Hübl is one of many real personages appearing in Kundera's fictional world. The fragments of real mingled with the fictional creates a cultural mosaic that poses a question about what is historical and fictional reality, the same question that arises vis-à-vis the photographs.

7. Similarly, according to Cadava, 85, Benjamin's theses "work to question those forms of pragmatism, positivism, and historicism that Benjamin understands as so many versions of a realism that establishes its truth by evoking the authority of so-called facts."

8. Not surprisingly, this statement has received some attention from the critics. Calvin Bedient, "On Milan Kundera," *Salmagundi* 73 (winter 1987): 97, for example, interprets it as the author's desire for "us to look with him into his heart and see the monster there, the one produced by 'the nonexistence of return.'" Misurella, 107, calls this scene "an autobiographical anecdote based on the transitory nature of our experience; because it happened once." At the same time, he stresses that even the narrator has limitations and nobody can understand everything. The introduction has a clear effect: we are reading fiction and not fact; the narrator reaches out to his readers on a human level, thus encouraging us to speculate along with him.

9. For example, both Maximilien Robespierre's French Revolution and the fourteenth-century war between two African kingdoms are considered in light of Nietzsche's "mad myth" of eternal return and at the same time intertwined into the twentieth-century Czech setting of the authorial I's World War II reminiscences. Discussions of the progressive cultural broadening in Kundera's works can be found in Misurella, 107; and Chvatík, *Svět románů Milana Kundery,* 78, 80, 81.

10. Although the Soviet invasion of Czechoslovakia is discussed in *The Book of Laughter and Forgetting,* it is not linked to photography.

11. In contrast, photographers are a target of ridicule in *Immortality* and in *Slowness.*

12. Susan Sontag, *On Photography* (New York: Farrar, Straus and Giroux, 1977), 5, notes that "photographs became a useful tool of modern states in the surveillance and control of their increasingly mobile populations" and were used for the first time in 1871 by the Paris police in the murderous roundup of Communards. It may not be only the fear of preservation that motivates the officer's severe response to Tereza; the scene suggests the power of photography to evoke the death of a subject. For more on the power of photography, see Cadava, 90. In *The Gift,* a family photograph is mentioned that depicts some members no longer living. Fyodor receives it from his mother as one of her most cherished possessions.

13. Tereza here is very much like Ganin at the end of Nabokov's *Mary.*

14. Sontag, 4. However, Sabina, who is presented throughout the text as emotionally strong, independent, and acutely intelligent, realizes the power play and is not willing to stay in her role for long. Unexpectedly, she reverses the situation by claiming the camera and ordering Tereza to strip; a command with which Tomas initiates an erotic situation, a command that is always obeyed. Interestingly, this sexually evocative power play brings the two women closer together, as symbolized by their laughter, a conclusion that Tomas would never

have predicted. O'Brien interprets this scene differently (see *MKF* 36–38, 121–22).

15. See the introduction, where I discuss Kundera's tightrope image in terms of Kafka's parable "The Bridge."

16. Tomas shares with Sabina this desire to unveil. He chooses his profession, which provides him with a double view: "Being a surgeon means slitting open the surface of things and looking at what lies hidden inside" (*ULB* 196).

17. Both Sabina's paintings and Tereza's photographs, exemplify a certain disjunctive, dislocating power, a power lost in which photographs have succumbed to ever-increasing technological perfection, and thus increasing mimetism, of contemporary photographs; see Cadava, 92.

18. I agree with John O'Brien's statement that the narrator's frequent intrusions "add to a certain thematic unity, but only in that they sometimes share a tangential connection; they do not contribute to an understanding as much as they are inconclusive in comparably similar ways"; in "Milan Kundera: Meaning, Play, and the Role of the Author," *Critique: Studies in Modern Fiction* 34, no. 1 (1992): 8.

19. Here the reader may recall Clementis, who was stripped of a hat, then of his life, and finally of a place in a photograph.

20. For more on the loss of individuality, see Misurella, 113.

21. See Jindřich Toman, "Glosa o Gottwaldově beranici a Kunderově stylu," *Proměny* 28 (1991): 33–35.

22. Cadava, 93.

23. Sontag, 23.

24. Kundera, *Art of the Novel*, 14.

25. Such formulaic novels can be compared to the kind of overly mimetic photography that loses its disjunctive power; see Cadava, 92.

26. Kundera, *Art of the Novel*, 14.

27. Susan Moore, "Kundera: The Massacre of Culture," *Quadrant*, April 1987, 63–66.

28. Catherine Fellows, "*The Unbearable Lightness of Being* on Film," in *Cinema and Fiction: New Modes of Adapting, 1950–1990*, ed. John Orr and Colin Nicholson (Edinburgh: Edinburgh University Press, 1992), 90.

29. Fellows, 91.

30. Květoslav Chvatík (in "Kunderova planeta nezkušenosti," in *Nesnesitelná lehkost bytí*, by Milan Kundera [Toronto: Sixty-eight, 1985], 286–87, the afterword to the Czech original of *The Unbearable Lightness of Being*) points out that the novel ends with an atmosphere of "smutné štěstí" (sad happiness) and wonders whether it is just a coincidence that a collection of poetry by the Czech poet Fráňa Šrámek bears the same title.

31. Genette, 67, states that advance notices are incompatible with suspense and for this reason appear rather infrequently in the Western tradition. In addition, because it seems more natural for the narrator

to allude to the future than for a character to do so, first-person narratives are better suited than other types of narrative to the use of advance notice.

32.   O'Brien (*MKF* 116) also links Sabina's pictorial art to Kundera's narrative art:

> Sabina's painting offers a clear alternative to oppositional thinking, and in that respect I believe Kundera presents Sabina's theory and practice of painting not only as a focal point of this novel, but also as a paradigm for understanding his work in general. Instead of reproducing surfaces that insist on a totalizing "intelligible lie," Kundera's novels, like Sabina's paintings, turn our attention to the deeper paradoxes, but not—and this is the most important point to make—at the expense of the surface representations. In this insistence on and dramatization/staging of double vision, Kundera's novels do not just invite deconstructionist perspective, but incorporate deconstructionist theory at the level of content.

33.   Kundera, *Art of the Novel,* 18–19.

Conclusion: *The Art of the Novel*

1.   Kundera, *Art of the Novel,* 18.
2.   Kafka, 430.
3.   Perhaps responsibility lies in not forgetting those who do not successfully expel demons and the place from which they came.
4.   Milan Kundera, *Testaments Betrayed: An Essay in Nine Parts,* trans. Linda Asher (New York: Harper Collins, 1995), 3.
5.   In this passage, Kundera, *Testaments Betrayed,* 5, links humor to the birth of the novel. Agreeing with Octavio Paz, he notes that "humor is an invention of the modern spirit." Humor, rarely discussed in Kundera or in Nabokov, certainly is a topic that requires its own study.
6.   Kundera, *Testaments Betrayed,* 4.
7.   This does not mean that Kundera's texts are meant to be interpreted in only one way. Kundera's narrators tend to present variations on the same theme, multiple perspectives, open-ended ideas, paradoxes, but these are not of a stylistic nature.
8.   The most elaborate stylistic feature Kundera indulges in is a musical structure. The tempo of individual chapters in his novels is directed by various musical compositions. Kundera offers comments on this feature in his essays on literature. See Kundera, "Dialogue on the Art of Composition," in *Art of the Novel,* 71–96.
9.   The enjoyable reading, which is by necessity nonlinear, recalls Roland Barthes's statement about his idea of a pleasurable reading process: it is not the narrative's "content or even its structure, but rather the abrasions I impose upon the fine surface: I read on, I skip, I look up, I dip in again." See, Barthes, *The Pleasure of the Text,* trans. Richard Miller (New York: Hill and Wang, 1975), 12.
10.   Barthes, *Pleasure of the Text,* 10.

11. This statement is in opposition to Kundera's critics who claim that he is trying to gain the Western audience.
12. See Bethea, "Style," 698.
13. Bethea notes that Nabokov's style challenges his critics to a better style as well; see "Style," 696.
14. Kundera, *Testaments Betrayed,* 160.

POSTSCRIPT

1. Kundera, *Testaments Betrayed,* 94.
2. Kundera, *Testaments Betrayed,* 95.

Bibliography

Aksyonov, Vassily. "Lungs and Gills." In *Altogether Elsewhere: Writers on Exile*. Ed. Marc Robinson. New York: Harcourt Brace, 1994. 234–37.

Alexandrov, Vladimir E. *Nabokov's Otherworld*. Princeton: Princeton University Press, 1991.

———, ed. *The Garland Companion to Vladimir Nabokov*. New York: Garland, 1995.

Banerjee, Maria Němcová. *Terminal Paradox: The Novels of Milan Kundera*. New York: Grove Weidenfield, 1990.

Barańczak, Stanisław. "Tongue-Tied Eloquence: Notes on Language, Exile, and Writing." In *Altogether Elsewhere: Writers on Exile*. Ed. Marc Robinson. New York: Harcourt Brace, 1994. 242–51.

Barthes, Roland. *Image-Music-Text*. Trans. Stephen Heath. New York: Hill and Wang, 1977.

———. *The Pleasure of the Text*. Trans. Richard Miller. New York: Hill and Wang, 1975.

Beaujour, Elizabeth Klosty. *Alien Tongues*. Ithaca: Cornell University Press, 1989.

Bedient, Calvin. "On Milan Kundera." *Salmagundi* 73 (winter 1987): 93–108.

Begnal, Michael. "Fiction, Biography, History: Nabokov's *The Gift*." *Journal of Narrative Techniques* 10, no. 2 (1980): 138–43.

Bergson, Henri. *Creative Evolution*. Trans. Arthur Mitchell. New York: University Press of America, 1983.

———. *Matter and Memory*. New York: Zone Books, 1988.

Bethea, David. *Joseph Brodsky and the Creation of Exile*. Princeton: Princeton University Press, 1995.

———. "Style." In *The Garland Companion to Vladimir Nabokov*. Ed. Vladimir E. Alexandrov. New York: Garland, 1995. 696–704.

Boyd, Brian. *Vladimir Nabokov: The Russian Years*. Princeton: Princeton University Press, 1990.

Boym, Svetlana. "Estrangement as a Lifestyle: Shklovsky and Brodsky." In *Exile and Creativity: Signposts, Travelers, Outsiders, Backward Glances*. Ed. Susan Rubin Suleiman. Durham: Duke University Press, 1998. 241–62.

Breytenbach, Breyten. "A Letter from Exile, to Don Espejuelo." In *Altogether Elsewhere: Writers on Exile*. Ed. Marc Robinson. New York: Harcourt Brace, 1994. 12–16.

Brodsky, Joseph. "The Condition We Call Exile." In *Altogether Elsewhere: Writers on Exile*. Ed. Marc Robinson. New York: Harcourt Brace, 1994. 3–11.

———. "Why Milan Kundera Is Wrong about Dostoyevsky." *Cross Currents* 5 (1986): 474–83.

Cadava, Eduardo. "Words of Light: Theses on the Photography of History." *Diacritics* 22, nos. 3–4 (1992): 84–114.

Chvatík, Květoslav. "Kunderova planeta nezkušenosti" In *Nesnesitelná lehkost bytí*. By Milan Kundera. Toronto: Sixty-eight, 1985. 285–92.

———. *Svět románů Milana Kundery*. Brno: Atlantis, 1994.

Clark, Katerina. *The Soviet Novel: History As Ritual*. Chicago: University of Chicago Press, 1981.

Connolly, Julian W. *Nabokov's Early Fiction: Patterns of Self and Other*. Cambridge: Cambridge University Press, 1992.

Conrad, Joseph. *A Personal Record: The Works of Joseph Conrad*. London: Dent Uniform Edition, 1946.

Corngold, Stanley. "Kafka's *Die Verwandlung*: Metamorphosis of the Metaphor." *Mosaic* 3 (summer 1970): 91–106.

Davydov, Sergei. "*The Gift*: Nabokov's Aesthetic Exorcism of Chernyshevskii." *Canadian-American Slavic Studies* 19, no. 3 (1985): 357–74.

———. "*Teksty-Matreshki*" *Vladimira Nabokova*. München: Verlag Otto Sagner, 1982.

———. "Weighing Nabokov's *Gift* on Pushkin's Scales." In *Cultural Mythologies of Russian Modernism: From the Golden Age to the Silver Age*. Ed. Boris Gasparov, Robert P. Hughes, and Irina Paperno. Berkeley: University of California Press, 1992. 415–28.

Dolinin, Alexander. "*The Gift*." In *The Garland Companion to Vladimir Nabokov*. Ed. Vladimir E. Alexandrov. New York: Garland, 1995. 135–65.

Eagle, Herbert. "Genre and Paradigm in Milan Kundera's *The Book of Laughter and Forgetting*." In *In Honor of Ladislav Matějka*. Ed. Lubomír Doležel. Ann Arbor: University of Michigan Press, 1984. 251–84.

Fellows, Catherine. "*The Unbearable Lightness of Being* on Film." In *Cinema and Fiction: New Modes of Adapting, 1950–1990*. Ed. John Orr and Colin Nicholson. Edinburgh: Edinburgh University Press, 1992. 73–92.

Foster, John Burt, Jr. *Nabokov's Art of Memory and European Modernism*. Princeton: Princeton University Press, 1993.

Genette, Gérard. *Narrative Discourse: An Essay in Method*. Trans. Jane E. Lewin. Ithaca: Cornell University Press, 1980.

Greenleaf, Monika. "Fathers, Sons, and Imposters: Pushkin's Trace in *The Gift*." *Slavic Review* 53 (spring 1994): 140–58.

Gross, Ruth V. "Fallen Bridge, Fallen Woman, Fallen Text." *Newsletter of the Kafka Society of America* 5, no. 1 (1981): 15–24.

Hoffman, Eva. "Obsessed with Words." In *Altogether Elsewhere: Writers on Exile*. Ed. Marc Robinson. New York: Harcourt Brace, 1994. 229–33.

Hyde, G. M. *Vladimir Nabokov: America's Russian Novelist*. London: Marion Boyars, 1977.

Iser, Wolfgang. "The Reading Process: A Phenomenological Approach." In *Reader-Response Criticism*. Ed. Jane P. Tompkins. Baltimore: Johns Hopkins University Press, 1980. 50–70.

Johnson, D. Barton. *Worlds in Regression: Some Novels of Vladimir Nabokov*. Ann Arbor: Ardis, 1985.

Johnson, Kurt, and Steve Coates. *Nabokov's Blues: The Scientific Odyssey of a Literary Genius*. Cambridge: Zoland Books, 1999.

Kafka, Franz. *The Complete Stories*. Ed. Nahum N. Glatzer. New York: Schocken Books, 1971.

Karges, Joann. *Nabokov's Lepidoptera: Genres and Genera*. Ann Arbor: Ardis, 1985.

Karlinsky, Simon. "Theme and Structure in Vladimir Nabokov's 'Krug.'" In *Russian Literature and American Critics*. Ed. Kenneth N. Brostrom. Ann Arbor: Department of Slavic Languages and Literatures, 1984. 243–47.

Koelb, Clayton. "The Turn of the Trope: Kafka's 'Die Brucke.'" *Modern Austrian Literature* 22, no. 1 (1989): 57–70.

Kristeva, Julia. "A New Type of Intellectual: The Dissident." In *The Kristeva Reader*. Ed. T. Moi. Oxford: Blackwell, 1986. 292–300.

Kundera, Milan. *The Art of the Novel*. Trans. Linda Asher. New York: Grove, 1988.

———. *The Book of Laughter and Forgetting*. Trans. Michael Henry Heim. New York: Harper and Row, 1984.

———. *Kniha smíchu a zapomnění*. Toronto: Sixty-eight, 1981.

———. *Nesnesitelná lehkost bytí*. Toronto: Sixty-eight, 1985.

———. *Slowness*. Trans. Linda Asher. New York: Harper Collins, 1996.

———. *Testaments Betrayed: An Essay in Nine Parts*. Trans. Linda Asher. New York: Harper Collins, 1995.

———. *The Unbearable Lightness of Being*. Trans. Michael Henry Heim. New York: Harper and Row, 1984.

Laursen, Eric. "Memory in Nabokov's *Mary*." *Russian Review* 55, no. 1 (1996): 55–64.

Le Grand, Eva. *Kundera; or, The Memory of Desire*. Trans. Lin Burman. Waterloo: Wilfrid Laurier University Press, 1999.

Lindroth, Colette. "Mirrors of the Mind: Kaufman Conquers Kundera." *Film-Literature Quarterly* 19, no. 4 (1991): 229–34.

Metzger, Bruce M., ed. *The Apocrypha of the Old Testament*. New York: Oxford University Press, 1965.

Miller, J. Hillis. *Fiction and Repetition*. Cambridge, Mass.: Harvard University Press, 1982.

Misurella, Fred. *Understanding Milan Kundera: Public Events, Private Affairs*. Columbia: University of South Carolina Press, 1993.

Moore, Susan. "Kundera: The Massacre of Culture." *Quadrant*, April 1987, 63–66.

Nabokov, Vladimir. *Ada.* New York: McGraw-Hill, 1969.

———. *Dar.* 1952. Reprint, Ann Arbor: Ardis, 1975.

———. *The Gift.* Trans. Michael Scammel with the collaboration of the author. New York: Vintage International, 1991.

———. *Mary.* Trans. Michael Glenny with the collaboration of the author. New York: Vintage International, 1989.

———. *Mashen'ka.* Berlin: Slovo, 1926.

———. *Nikolay Gogol.* Norfolk: New Directions, 1944.

———. *Speak, Memory.* New York: G. P. Putnam's Sons, 1966.

O'Brien, John. *Milan Kundera and Feminism.* New York: St. Martin's, 1995.

———. "Milan Kundera: Meaning, Play, and the Role of the Author." *Critique: Studies in Modern Fiction* 34, no. 1 (1992): 3–18.

Paperno, Irina. "Kak sdelan '*Dar*' Nabokova." *Novoe Literaturnoe Obozrenie* 5 (1993): 138–55.

Parker, Stephen Jan. *Understanding Vladimir Nabokov.* Columbia: University of South Carolina Press, 1987.

Petro, Peter, ed. *Critical Essays on Milan Kundera.* New York: G. K. Hall, 1994.

Píchová, Hana. "The Bowler Hat as a Monument to Time Past in Milan Kundera's *The Unbearable Lightness of Being.*" *European Studies Journal* 14, no. 2 (1997): 5–19.

———. "The Narrator in Milan Kundera's *The Unbearable Lightness of Being.*" *Slavic and East European Journal* 36, no. 2 (1992): 217–26.

Píchová, Hana, and Marjorie E. Rhine. "Kundera's Kafka and Kafka's Kundera." *Modern Czech Studies* 11 (1999): 65–73.

Raeff, Marc. *Russia Abroad: A Cultural History of the Russian Emigration, 1919–1939.* Oxford: Oxford University Press, 1990.

Rimmon-Kenan, Shlomith. *Narrative Fiction: Contemporary Poetics.* London: Routledge, 1989.

Robinson, Fred Miller. "The History and Significance of the Bowler Hat: Chaplin, Laurel and Hardy, Beckett, Magritte, and Kundera." *Tri-Quarterly* 66 (spring–summer 1986): 173–200.

Robinson, Marc, ed. *Altogether Elsewhere: Writers on Exile.* New York: Harcourt Brace, 1994.

Said, Edward. "The Mind of Winter: Reflection on Life in Exile." *Harper's,* September 1984, 49–55.

Salomon, Roger B. "*The Gift*: Nabokov's Portrait of the Artist." In *Critical Essays on Vladimir Nabokov.* Ed. Phyllis A. Roth. Boston: G. K. Hall, 1984. 185–201.

Seidel, Michael. *Exile and the Narrative Imagination.* New Haven: Yale University Press, 1986.

Sicker, Philip. "Practicing Nostalgia: Time and Memory in Nabokov's Early Russian Fiction." *Studies in 20th Century Literature* 11, no. 2 (1987): 253–70.

Sontag, Susan. *On Photography.* New York: Farrar, Straus and Giroux, 1977.

Straus, Nina Pelikan. "Erasing History and Deconstructing the Text: Milan Kundera's *The Book of Laughter and Forgetting.*" *Critique: Studies in Modern Fiction* 28 (1987): 69–85.

Struve, Gleb. "Russian Writers in Exile: Problems of an Émigré Literature." *Comparative Literature* 2 (1958): 592–606.

Suleiman, Susan Rubin, ed. *Exile and Creativity: Signposts, Travelers, Outsiders, Backward Glances.* Durham: Duke University Press, 1998.

Tabori, Paul. *The Anatomy of Exile: A Semantic and Historical Study.* London: Harrap, 1972.

Toker, Leona. *Nabokov: The Mystery of Literary Structures.* Ithaca: Cornell University Press, 1989.

Toman, Jindřich. "Glosa o Gottwaldove beranici a Kunderove stylu." *Proměny* 28 (1991): 33–35.

Index

achronology, 106
Ada (Nabokov), 114, 119n. 6
Aksyonov, Vassily, 7
Alexandrov, Vladimir, 32–33, 85, 111,
  112, 123n. 30
allegory, 53–54
anthill metaphor, 34, 35, 42
Apocrypha, 51–52
artistic issues: in *The Gift,* 29–33, 37–
  39, 42–45, 76–78, 84–85, 123n.
  25; in *The Unbearable Lightness of
  Being,* 55–56, 59–60, 136n. 32
Art of the Novel, The (Kundera), 129n.
  32

balance, 2–7, 96–97; memory and,
  42–43, 63, 109
Banerjee, Maria Němcová, 51, 126n. 4
Barańczak, Stanisław, 8, 9, 110
Barthes, Roland, 112, 136n. 9
Bedient, Calvin, 134n. 8
Begnal, Michael, 132n. 22
Benjamin, Walter, 107, 134n. 7
Bergson, Henri, 20, 61–62, 119n. 9
Bethea, David, 120n. 13
biblical references, 51–52, 64–65
blindness, imagery of, 72–73, 75, 83–84
Book of Laughter and Forgetting, The
  (Kundera), 9; allegory in, 53–54;
  biblical references in, 51–52; dia-
  ries in, 53–54, 126nn. 2, 3; forget-
  ting in, 46–47, 51–53, 62, 127n.
  18; photography in, 88–92, 98–
  100, 102–3; privacy in, 47–49, 54;
  silencing in, 49–50, 57, 60–61,
  130n. 6; structure of narrative in,
  50, 127n. 7
Book of Tobit, 51–52
Boyd, Brian, 28, 31, 34–35, 44, 79

Breytenbach, Breyten, 8
"Bridge, The" (Kafka), 1–6
bridge metaphor, 2, 4–6, 52, 75–76,
  88, 113
Brodsky, Joseph, 3, 67, 69
bureaucracy, 73–74
butterfly imagery: in *The Gift,* 32–45,
  82, 84, 123n. 31, 123–24n. 32,
  124n. 34; in *Mary,* 25–27, 122nn.
  16, 17

Cadava, Eduardo, 102, 132–33n. 1,
  133n. 2, 134n. 7
Cambodia, 94
Cervantes, Miguel de, 107, 108–9
Chaplin, Charlie, 56–57
Chekhov, Anton, 70
Chernyshevsky, Nikolay, 77–78, 84,
  86–87, 130n. 9, 131n. 14
chess imagery, 78, 131n. 18
Chvatík, Květoslav, 135n. 30
Clementis, Vladimir, 88–91, 102,
  133n. 5, 135n. 18
Connolly, Julian, 20, 21, 38–39, 70,
  80, 121n. 8
contrapuntal vision, 6–7, 9, 39, 120n.
  13
creativity, 21–22, 108–9
critical distance, 39, 85–86
cultural differences, 8, 48–49
cultural memory, 10–12, 30, 69, 121n.
  23; artistic issues and, 76–77; in
  The Gift, 12–13, 30, 76–87; historical moments and, 88–90; in
  Mary, 69–76; rewriting history
  and, 90–91. *See also* memory; personal memory; photography
Czechoslovak Communist Party, 88–
  90

145

Hana Píchová was born in Prague, Czechoslovakia, and came to the United States in 1980. Presently, she is an associate professor of Slavic languages and literature at the University of Texas at Austin, where she teaches literature and the Czech language.